STRINGER LAWRENCE

STRINGER LAWRENCE

THE FATHER OF THE INDIAN ARMY

By COLONEL J. BIDDULPH

GYAN

Published by

GYAN

Gyan Publishing House
5, Ansari Road
Daryaganj, New Delhi-110002
Phone: 011-47034999, 9811692060
E-mail: books@gyanbooks.com

Distribution Network
gyanbooks.com
India, USA, Canada, UK, Australia

ISBN: 978-93-6208-194-0 (PB)
First Published, 1901

2nd Impression 2024

Printed at: Gyan Press, Delhi.

STRINGER LAWRENCE
Author: COLONEL J. BIDDULPH

After Sir Joshua Reynolds.

Stringer Lawrence

STRINGER LAWRENCE

THE FATHER OF THE INDIAN ARMY

BY COLONEL J. BIDDULPH

INDIAN STAFF CORPS

AUTHOR OF "THE NINETEENTH AND THEIR TIMES"

LONDON

JOHN MURRAY, ALBEMARLE STREET

1901

CONTENTS

CHAPTER IV.

Defence of Madras

PREFACE

THE object of this Memoir is to rescue from oblivion the name of a soldier to whom the British Empire owes a great debt of gratitude. We have been so long accustomed to consider ourselves as the only European nation in India, that it is apt to be forgotten how great was French predominance, in that country, in the middle of the eighteenth century. When Lawrence went to India, with no higher commission than to command a small undisciplined garrison of two or three hundred men, our tenure in India hung by a thread. With few troops and scanty resources, under conditions of warfare novel to him, Lawrence gave check to the ambitious schemes of Dupleix, established the prestige of English arms, and secured time for the English Ministry to recognise the importance of the unofficial war that was being waged by the East India Company against

France. Lawrence was the second and the most distinguished of the little band of English officers whose services were transferred from the Crown to the Company, and who wrote their names so deeply in the history of our earlier wars in India. He was also the first English Commander-in-Chief in India. Nor was Lawrence's merit confined to his services in the field. By his good judgment, unfailing common sense and uprightness of character, he secured the confidence of his masters in England and of his colleagues in India to a degree that no others of his time were able to attain. Alone among his contemporaries, he stands distinguished as the only man in a prominent position whom no voice of dislike or malice ever assailed.

Some account of his operations round Trichinopoly has been given by Lawrence himself; but with characteristic modesty he has told his story so briefly as almost to deprive it of interest. Orme's history contains a detailed account of Lawrence's campaigns, but they are intermingled with such a mass of details in which Lawrence was not concerned, that Lawrence's own personality is lost sight of.

The dates given in this Memoir, up to

3rd September, 1752, are according to Old Style.

The tables of the rulers of the Deccan and the Carnatic, in the eighteenth century, given in Appendix, serve to show how the appointed Governors first became independent of Delhi, and, in time, founded lines of hereditary rulers.

LIST OF ILLUSTRATIONS

STRINGER LAWRENCE

I.

FIRST SERVICE IN INDIA

In these days when the most trifling skirmish is telegraphed to all parts of the world, when the distribution of medals and rewards is discussed before a campaign is ended, it is somewhat difficult to realise the small notice that has been taken of some of the men who laid the foundations of our Indian Empire in the eighteenth century. Clive and Coote have found their niche in the temple of Fame; but, besides them, there were a number of officers, not inferior to them in military achievement, who, as majors and captains, often only as subalterns, commanded armies in the field, won important victories, conducted sieges, and carried on successful operations during a long series of years, generally against superior numbers, always under great difficulties, whose names have almost passed into oblivion: "stout-hearted but utterly forgotten Englishmen, who, at great odds and with small means, sustained the fortunes of their country in many a hazardous predicament by their devoted bravery and steadfast perseverance." Some of their deeds have been chronicled by Orme; but Orme is only to be read by the few. Without some personal knowledge of India he cannot be read to much advantage. There is no skimming or dipping into Orme. His long-drawn narrative of fifteen years' warfare, diffused and monotonous, merges its interest in a multiplicity of personages and details among which all sense of proportion is lost. The enemies against whom our armies contended were no contemptible foes. In statesmanship and far-reaching views there was nobody in authority on the English side who could match Dupleix, while he was in India. He was, through the greater part of his career, well supported by his own Government, and wielded resources that his English opponents never commanded. Fortunately he was no soldier. La Bourdonnais, Bussy and Lally were excellent generals. They were less hampered by their own local Government than were the English commanders, who were continually subjected to vexatious interference in military details. The French troops were more numerous and better equipped than the English. The native commanders pitted against us were frequently bad, though Hyder Ali was as fine a military leader as India has ever produced; but the numbers and resources they could bring into the field made them very formidable. The fighting was often of a most desperate nature. If there was any superiority of arms it was not on our side. The native chiefs had strong fortresses, powerful trains of artillery, and thousands of horsemen, against which our people were obliged to match themselves with slow-moving infantry and a few field pieces drawn by oxen. Sepoys were enlisted and disciplined by the French, before the idea was taken up by the English. Our Sepoys, at first, had only such weapons as they could themselves furnish; sometimes only bows and arrows, and spears. It was not till the end of 1754 that the first regiment of the British army landed in India. Before that date, the Company had to depend on the sweepings of the English seaports, gathered by sharks and crimps; for they were not allowed to recruit openly. Orme describes a newly-arrived batch in 1752, the very men with whom Clive took Covelong and Chingleput, as being "as usual, the refuse of the vilest employments in London."* Sometimes Swiss mercenaries were obtained, who deserted wholesale and enlisted in the French ranks. Such one-sided combats as the superior armaments of our day have rendered possible† never fell to the lot of our armies in India in the eighteenth century. Our successes in India were largely due to the fine qualities of our subordinate officers when entrusted with detached commands. This was where the inferiority of the French showed itself. Equal to us on other points, and our superiors in many, their subordinate officers proved themselves markedly inferior to the English, when confronted with unexpected difficulties, or when acting independently. Nor did French officers succeed in developing the best qualities of their

* Clive, in 1758, writes with reference to the King's intention to give him a Colonel's commission :—"I shall never make any use of it, for I am not at all inclined to enter the lists with Monsieur Lally. Experience, discipline and perhaps bravery would be against me. For you well know the men which come to India are the worst of their kind, and surely the best men of France are equal to the worst men of England."

† On the 8th May, 1866, at Irdjar, a Russian force of about 3,000 men defeated 40,000 Bokhara troops, having only 12 men wounded.

Sepoys, to the same degree that English officers were able to do. While our regular forces were engaged in Germany and America, our first successes in India were, to a great extent, won by our waifs and strays, by the younger sons of younger sons, the failures and ne'er-do-weels who went to India in search of a career that they were unable to find at home.

The capture of Madras by the French, in September, 1746, was the beginning of our military career in India. At that time, the few European soldiers in the East India Company's service were merely factory guards, with little organisation and less discipline. After nearly one hundred and fifty years of existence, the Company was still a purely trading association; trade, not territory, was their object, and they had steadily kept aloof from interference in local politics. The declaration of war, by France, found the Companies of both nations equally unprepared for hostilities. On the appearance of an English squadron, under Commodore Barnet, off the Coromandel Coast, in 1745, Dupleix, the French Governor of Pondicherry, prevailed on the Nawab of the Carnatic to prohibit hostilities, and Barnet sailed away.

The English Company, secure in the Nawab's assurance that he would force the French to observe a similar neutrality, took no precautions to strengthen themselves. When, therefore, a French squadron, under La Bourdonnais, appeared off Madras, in September, 1746, no resistance was possible. Dupleix had secured the neutrality of the Nawab, by promising to put him in possession of Madras, and the place fell after two days' bombardment. The garrison, at that time, consisted only of some 200 Europeans fit for duty and about three thousand Peons, less than a third of whom were armed with muskets. The officers were three lieutenants, two of whom were foreigners, and seven ensigns promoted from the ranks. Only one lieutenant and one ensign were deemed efficient officers.

The Nawab, as soon as he found that Dupleix was playing him false, and had no intention of surrendering Madras to him, sent his son, Mahfoos Khan, with ten thousand men to expel the French. The French, under M. Paradis, inflicted a bloody defeat on the Nawab's army, at S. Thomé, six weeks after the capture of Madras from the English, which practically made Dupleix dictator of the

Carnatic. A few weeks later he succeeded in making terms with the Nawab, and was left in peace to prosecute his plans against the English.

The Directors in London, thinking only of trade, took no steps to strengthen Madras till after it had fallen. Major Knipe, the commander of the Fort St. George garrison, had died in May, 1743; after much delay Captain Stringer Lawrence was selected to succeed him. Little is known of Lawrence's parentage.* He was the son of John Lawrence and Mary his wife, of Hereford, where he was born on the 24th February, 1697–8. In December, 1727, he received a commission, as ensign, in Major-General Clayton's regiment, now the West Yorkshire, and saw service with that regiment in Spain and Flanders, and during the Highland rising of 1745. He became a lieutenant in March, 1735–6, captain in June, 1745, and retired on 20th January, 1746–7. The circumstances under which his services were transferred to the East India Company are not known; but it was not till the Company had agreed to employ him that his name ceased to appear on the rolls of Clayton's regiment.

* *See* Appendix.

According to the record of the Directors' Proceedings for 17th December, 1746, it was "Resolved that the garrison of Fort St. George be strengthened with a number of recruits, sergeants, and ensigns, and that an able officer be sent from hence, as Major thereof, at the salary of £250 per annum and one hundred guineas for his charges out. And Captain Lawrence being recommended as a person qualified for the post, Resolved by the Ballot that the said Captain Lawrence be appointed Major of the Garrison on the terms above mentioned, and, being called in, he was acquainted therewith." On the 18th February following, when he was forty-nine years of age, he took the usual oath, and sailed in the *Winchelsea*. His appointment was notified to the Governor of Madras in the following terms:—"Stringer Lawrence, Esq., is entertained by us to be Major of our Garrison at Fort St. George upon the same terms as Major Knipe, viz.: two hundred and fifty pounds sterling per annum and one of the Companies." About one hundred and fifty men embarked at the same time. It is noteworthy that the views of the Directors, at that time, were limited to strengthening the Fort St. George garrison.

The idea of using troops in the field, or for any other purpose than defending their own walls, had never entered their minds.

Four months after Lawrence's departure the news of the fall of Madras reached London. The English at Madras having all been taken prisoners, the Directors appointed a new governor, and a Council, of which Lawrence was made the third member; but it was ordered that his work in the Council was to be confined to military advice and duties.

Lawrence's voyage lasted nearly eleven months. For some reason his ship went to Batavia, before making the Coromandel coast. Probably they received news of the fall of Madras at the Cape, and went to Batavia to await further intelligence.

In January, 1748, Lawrence landed at Fort St. David, then momentarily expecting an attack by the French. After the fall of Madras, the Fort St. David officials had taken on themselves the administration of the Company's affairs on the coast. Very little was then wanting to deprive the English of their last foothold in Southern India. Two attacks, since the fall of Madras, had been foiled rather than defeated. Lawrence's first care was to form a camp outside the walls. This led to the detection of a plot among the native officers of Peons, who were in secret correspondence with Dupleix. The presence of the English fleet on the coast prevented any French movement against the place for a time. Lawrence employed the interval in reorganising the companies of Europeans, and introducing a system of military law. The reorganised companies were seven in number, consisting each of one captain, one lieutenant, one ensign, four sergeants, four corporals, three drummers, and seventy privates. The lieutenant of Lawrence's company was called captain-lieutenant, and ranked as a captain. In the field, these companies acted together as a battalion, but ten years elapsed before they were formed into an administrative battalion in quarters. In the same way, the Peons were organised in companies, and, eleven years later, in battalions. It was in such humble beginnings that the Anglo-Indian army had its origin.

Six months after Lawrence's arrival, Dupleix took advantage of the absence of the British squadron to make another attempt against Cuddalore. By a sudden march, a force of eight hundred Europeans and one thousand Sepoys, from Pondicherry, appeared within three miles of Cuddalore on the morning of the 17th June. Lawrence had intelligence of the design, and ostentatiously withdrew the guns and garrison to Fort St. David, about a mile distant, giving out that he did not consider Cuddalore tenable. Directly night fell, he marched back the garrison and guns. At midnight the French advanced with scaling ladders, and were received with such a fire of grape and musketry that they flung down their arms and retreated precipitately to Pondicherry without making any further attempt. Two months later, Lawrence was involved in a disaster of the same nature as he had inflicted on the French.

On receipt of the news of the loss of Madras, the Directors in London were roused to action. Being devoid of military resources, their application to the Crown for assistance met with a ready response. An expedition, against Pondicherry, was fitted out under Admiral Boscawen, and sailed from England in November, 1747. For the purposes of the expedition, twelve independent companies, each of one hundred rank and file, were formed by drafts from different regiments. A force of artillery was added, and the whole force consisted of about 1,400 men. Some time was wasted in an abortive attempt against Mauritius. On the 29th July, the squadron arrived off Fort St. David: the troops were landed, and, on 8th August, began their march to Pondicherry. The whole of the operations by land and sea were in Boscawen's hands, and the miscarriage of affairs was ascribed to his ignorance of land warfare. With marines, sailors, and a Dutch contingent from Negapatam, the European rank and file amounted to 3,720 men. Lawrence's authority only extended to the Company's troops, which formed a fifth of the whole force, not counting Sepoys.

The first attempt was made against Ariancopang, a detached fort two miles from Pondicherry. Without information, without reconnaissance, and without scaling ladders, seven hundred men were marched to the attack, with the inevitable consequences. One hundred and fifty men were killed or wounded, the best officer among the English troops being among the killed, without the slightest advantage being gained. It was found necessary to commence regular siege operations against Ariancopang.

After much blundering, a battery was opened with very little effect. M. Law, who commanded in Ariancopang, made a sudden sortie, with a mixed force of infantry and cavalry, against a part of the entrenchment held by sailors. The sailors were struck with panic at the sight of the cavalry, and fled. The panic communicated itself to the regular troops, and the whole of the entrenchment was abandoned. Lawrence, who commanded in the trenches that day, disdained to fly, and was made prisoner. The same day the magazine in the fort was blown up by accident, forcing the garrison to retreat into Pondicherry.

On the 30th August, Boscawen broke ground before Pondicherry. Blunder was heaped upon blunder, till, at the end of a month, during which no progress was made, it was found necessary to abandon the siege. One thousand and sixty-five soldiers and sailors had perished, and an enormous quantity of ammunition had been uselessly expended. "There are very few instances of late years," Orme remarks, "of a siege carried on by the English with less skill than this of Pondicherry." In November, news was received of the cessation of arms in Europe. Lawrence was permitted to return to Fort St.

David on parole, pending ratification of the treaty of Aix-la-Chapelle, which restored Madras to the English.

The establishment of peace left both English and French stronger in military resources in India than they had ever been before. The French profited by the occasion to mingle in the politics of the Deccan and Carnatic courts; a step destined to increase enormously their political influence, and to force the English into opposition. On the English side, Boscawen, burning to retrieve his failure against Pondicherry, by some notable exploit, agreed with the Company's officials to espouse the cause of a Tanjore prince who had been living for some years under the Company's protection. This Tanjore claimant was profuse in his promises to the English, and in his assurances that his appearance in Tanjore territory at the head of an armed force would be the signal for thousands to join his standard. In return for assistance in gaining the throne of Tanjore, he undertook to cede Devicotah to the English. At the end of March, 1749, four hundred and thirty Europeans, with a thousand Sepoys and a small siege train were despatched against

Devicotah, under command of Captain Cope. The force reached Devicotah with only three days' provisions in hand, and, after a series of blundering operations in which the troops were only saved from destruction by a want of enterprise on the part of the Tanjoreans, Cope was glad to make his way back to Fort St. David. The English were by this time disillusioned as to the influence of their *protégé*, but thought it necessary to wipe out the reproach of their failure by a second expedition, which was entrusted to Lawrence.

This time success crowned their efforts. The details of the capture possess little interest beyond the fact that it was on this occasion that Clive first came prominently under Lawrence's notice. A breach had been made, and Clive volunteered to lead the storming party. The Sepoys held back, and Clive's little party of Europeans was cut to pieces; Clive himself being almost the only one that escaped. Lawrence at once made a second assault at the head of his whole European force, and Devicotah fell. The Tanjore ruler was glad to make peace, on account of the changes produced in the Carnatic by French intrigues, and Devicotah was ceded to the

English. The acquisition of Devicotah was not a very creditable business for the Company. It was their first deliberate attempt at territorial acquisition, without the excuse of acting in self-defence. Having gained their object, they threw over the Tanjore prince whose claims they had affected to assert. The prime mover in the business appears to have been Boscawen.

Boscawen, who had only waited on the coast till Madras was received from the French, returned to England. Lawrence was appointed, by the Directors, Chief Commissioner to take over Madras. Many of the survivors of the troops Boscawen had brought out with him entered the service of the Company. Eleven subalterns were in this way transferred to the Company's service, their names being retained on the half-pay list in the event of their returning to England at a future date. Among them may be mentioned two officers, John Dalton and James Kilpatrick, who served in India with much distinction.

In spite of peace having been established in Europe, the English and French in India were soon again opposed to each other in the field. Rival claimants were contending for the thrones of the Deccan and the Carnatic, and the real issue of the struggle depended on the English and French commanders; though they only appeared as auxiliaries in the rival camps. In March, 1750, Lawrence, with six hundred Europeans, joined the camp of Nazir Jung, the Soobadar of the Deccan, who was opposed by the rival pretenders to the Soobahship and the Nawabship of the Carnatic, supported by a force of 2,000 French under d'Auteuil, the brother-in-law of Dupleix. It was the first time, since the establishment of peace, that English and French troops had been opposed to each other, and d'Auteuil tried to intimidate Lawrence by a bit of bluff. Sending him a flag of truce, he expressed his desire that no European blood should be shed. As he did not know where the English were posted, he would not be to blame if any shot came in their direction. Lawrence replied that his post would be known by the English colours carried on his flag-gun; that he too, was averse to spilling European blood, but if any shot came his way he would certainly return them. In order to try Lawrence's mettle, d'Auteuil fired a shot over the English camp. Lawrence at once answered it with three guns, "and saw they were well pointed."

d'Auteuil, with a mutiny amongst his men, thought so badly of his prospects that he retreated the same night, sacrificing his guns and artillerymen. But Lawrence's relations with Nazir Jung were so unsatisfactory that he shortly afterwards left him, and marched his troops to Madras.

At this time important changes took place among the officials at Madras. Floyer, the governor, and Holt, the next in seniority to him, were dismissed from the service; Saunders was summoned from Vizagapatam to assume charge at Madras, and, for four months, Lawrence was made provisional governor of Fort St. David. Before Mr. Saunders' arrival, Lawrence's relations with the provisional Government at Madras became strained. He had cause of dissatisfaction in regard to several matters. The Company's practice permitted interference in the most trifling military details by the civil officers whose business it was to manage the Company's trade. In June, 1748, the power to convene court martials had been granted to Lawrence by the Directors, though the power of overriding them was vested in the Governor and Council. In 1750, the Court of Directors sent orders for the withdrawal of Lawrence's powers; but it was found impracticable to do this. He was also dissatisfied at the failure of the Company to enforce necessary measures for the maintenance of discipline. He had no proper authority over his men, and his pay was miserably small. On the 25th September, he resigned the Company's service, and sailed for England a month later.

The Directors acted with a sagacity that they did not always show in similar circumstances. They packed Lawrence back to India before he had been two months in England, with the appointment of Commander-in-Chief of all the Company's military forces in the East Indies, on a salary of £500 per annum, to which was added a yearly allowance of £250 "in lieu of diet money, servants, horses, and all other privileges and perquisites whatever." He was also commissioned to consider at once of the proper establishment for forming a company of artillery at Fort St. George. The most stirring part of Lawrence's career was about to commence.

II.

TRICHINOPOLY

On the 14th March, 1752, Lawrence again landed in Madras, and at once took command of the army that was about to march under Clive. At this time a Political Committee of the Council was formed for the first time. It consisted of three members, of whom Lawrence was one. During his absence, the unofficial war between the English and French Companies, acting as auxiliaries of the rival claimants to the Nawabship of the Carnatic, had been prosecuted with vigour, and Clive had sprung into notice by his feats at Arcot and Covripauk. During Lawrence's absence a dangerous spirit of discontent had arisen among the officers, owing to a breach of faith, on the part of Government, affecting their allowances, and the whole discipline of the troops was very bad. Three days after landing, Lawrence, with 1,500 men, of whom 400 were Europeans, marched to the relief of Trichinopoly, where Mahomed Ali, the English claimant to the Nawabship, with a small English force under Captains de Gingens and Dalton, had been besieged, for seven months, by a French force under M. Law, the French officer into whose hands Lawrence had fallen prisoner at Ariancopang, and a large native force under Chunda Sahib, the French claimant. In Trichinopoly also was a Mahratta force under Morari Rao, the chief of Gooti, in the pay of Mysore, and a contingent from Tanjore, whose ruler had, for the time, cast in his lot with Mahomed Ali. On the 26th March, Lawrence arrived within twenty miles of Trichinopoly. Morari Rao was, at this time, in secret correspondence with the French, an advantage to Law of which Lawrence was ignorant. Law and Chunda Sahib were encamped on the south bank of the Cauvery, about five miles east of Trichinopoly. It was of the utmost importance to them to prevent the junction of Lawrence's force with the garrison. Several favourable positions were open to Law for opposing Lawrence's march, at the different rivers Lawrence was obliged to cross before arrival within striking distance of the besieged town; but Law neglected his opportunities. Instead of moving to meet Lawrence, he left the issue to be decided on the ground on which he stood. Ten miles from the allied camp, Law had occupied Coiladdy, where the Cauvery divides into several branches, with about six hundred men, and had formed there a formidable battery commanding Lawrence's route at point blank range. Lawrence's march was directed along the strip of land between the two southern branches of the Cauvery, whereby a certain amount of protection was afforded to his convoy. It was his intention to strike southwards across the southernmost branch, before coming in touch with Coiladdy: but his guides misled him, and he suddenly found himself under the fire of the battery. Twenty Europeans were killed, and much confusion caused among the baggage before he could extricate himself. Continuing his march, without further interruption, Lawrence halted that night about ten miles from Trichinopoly.

The next morning, 28th March, Lawrence resumed his march, having been joined in the night by a hundred Europeans and fifty dragoons from the garrison. While he directed his march on the fortified rock of Elmiseram, another detachment from the garrison, under

Captain Dalton, consisting of two hundred Europeans and four hundred Sepoys with four guns, took post at the Sugarloaf Rock. Law had drawn up his force, with his right resting on Elmiseram, and his left thrown back to the Cauvery at Chucklipolliam. Lawrence's business was to reach Trichinopoly, not to fight a general action; so, directing his march southwards, he marched round Elmiseram, and was joined by Dalton at noon. Here a halt was called, to rest the troops who were suffering greatly from the heat, while Morari Rao and his Mahrattas from the city pretended to skirmish with the French. Soon, news was received that the whole French line, with their allies, were advancing. Lawrence at once pushed forward Clive with a small detachment of Europeans and some guns, to occupy some buildings that Law had neglected to occupy, while he moved up, in order, to his support. A fierce cannonade ensued, from nine guns on the English side against twenty-two on the French. The English troops were well sheltered, while the Frenchmen stood without cover on the open plain. In half an hour they wavered and gave ground, withdrawing their guns. Clive and Dalton followed them up till they took refuge in the watercourse near French Rock. Here they would have been exposed to a severe enfilading fire, when Lawrence, satisfied with the advantage he had gained, and unwilling to overtax the energies of his men, who were suffering severely from the heat, ordered the pursuit to cease. He was also, no doubt, influenced by the dubious behaviour of Morari Rao. Seven of his Europeans had died of sunstroke, and fourteen were killed or disabled by the cannonade. The French losses were heavier. They had lost about forty Europeans, while some three hundred of their native allies, about the same number of horses, and an elephant lay dead on the field. The commander of Chunda Sahib's cavalry had also been killed.

Continuing his march, Lawrence entered Trichinopoly the same evening. On the night of the 1st April, he sent Dalton with four hundred men to beat up the French camp, and set fire to it. Dalton lost his way, but managed to regain Trichinopoly without loss, though morning had surprised him in the midst of the French posts. The mere attempt alarmed Law to such an extent that he precipitately withdrew across the south branch of

TRICHINOPOLY.

[To face p. 34.

the Cauvery, on to the Island of Seringham,* destroying a quantity of stores he was unable to take with him. The next day, Lawrence sent Dalton with a small force against Elmiseram, an isolated rock with a fortified temple on the summit. A small party of grenadiers, attempting a night attack without orders, were beaten back, but the place surrendered on the following morning. Fifteen Frenchmen, thirty Sepoys, and two guns, one of them an 18-pounder, were captured. Two days afterwards, Dalton and the grenadiers captured another gun. Law had posted a gun in a small building on the island, commanding the bathing place used by the principal leaders of Mahomed Ali's army. Dalton concealed his men behind an old wall on the bank of the river. At noon, when the guard were asleep or engaged in cooking, the grenadiers forded the river and captured the gun, before it could be fired twice. The gun was brought across the river, under cover of some field pieces that had been sent to cover their retreat. The boldness and success of these achievements made an impression on both sides, out of all proportion to their importance. Hitherto, the

* Sri Runghum.

operations of the English had been feeble and wanting in resolution, with the exception of Clive's deeds at Arcot and Covripauk, while the French had carried all before them. Now the French were forced into a defensive attitude, and the English were the attackers. Among the first results was a change in the behaviour of Morari Rao, who relinquished for a time his treacherous correspondence with Chunda Sahib. Law's position on the island was an extremely strong one. After experience showed that it was almost unassailable, owing to the hollow ways and watercourses with which the ground of the island was intersected, and to the great stone temples, standing in walled enclosures, which could be converted into defensible posts. The only necessity of Law's position was that he should keep open his communications with Pondicherry.

Clive, whom Lawrence had taken into his confidence, now made the daring proposal to divide the army, sending one half of it north of the Cauvery to intercept Law's communications with Pondicherry. Hazardous as such a move would have been in face of an enterprising foe, Lawrence at once agreed to it. By this time he had gauged Law's want of enterprise, while recognising his own advantage in possessing such a coadjutor as Clive. His superiority in cavalry, at this time, an advantage he never again possessed, made the division of his army less hazardous than it would otherwise have been. On the scheme being made known to Lawrence's native allies, they declared that they would take no part in it, unless Clive was given the detached command. Some anxiety was felt by Lawrence, who had intended to give the command to Clive, lest the officers senior to Clive should decline to serve under him; and it is a proof of the good spirit Lawrence was able to infuse into his officers that no demur was made.

On the night of the 6th April, Clive, with four hundred Europeans, seven hundred Sepoys, four thousand native horse, and eight guns, passed the Cauvery, and occupied Samiaveram, where they entrenched themselves. As a counter-move, Law sent a party to occupy Munserpet. A detachment sent by Clive to dislodge them was repulsed with some loss. But the enemy was faint-hearted, and retired to Pitchandah. Clive followed up his advantage by capturing Lalgoodi, where Law had a large magazine of supplies.

Meanwhile, Dupleix, greatly alarmed at the situation produced by Law's retreat to Seringham, had collected all the men he could spare from Pondicherry, and sent them, under d'Auteuil, to reinforce Law. d'Auteuil reached Ootatoor, thirteen miles north-east of Samiaveram, on the 14th April, and sent messengers to Law advising him of his intention to reach the Cauvery by a circuitous night march. One of his messengers was captured by Clive, who marched the same night to intercept him. d'Auteuil received news of Clive's march, and fell back on Ootatoor. Clive also returned to Samiaveram. Clive's movement to intercept d'Auteuil was known to Law on the following day; but not his return. Law at once detached a small party of eighty Europeans, forty of whom were English deserters, and seven hundred Sepoys to surprise Clive's camp at Samiaveram, while he was engaged with d'Auteuil. They reached Clive's camp at midnight, and, by the help of the English deserters, passed themselves off on Clive's Sepoys as a reinforcement from Lawrence. The story was believed; they were conducted through the camp, and, on reaching Clive's quarters, opened fire on the buildings in which Clive and his soldiers were asleep. There ensued five or six hours of extraordinary confusion, in the course of which Clive had several wonderful escapes. Twice he was alone in the midst of the enemy, mistaking them for his own men ; but his courage and presence of mind saved him. A third time he was treacherously fired at while parleying with the enemy, who had taken post in the building in which he had been sleeping at the time of attack, and the two men on whom he was leaning were killed. Daylight made the French aware of the failure of their attempt, and they surrendered. The French Sepoys, attempting to retreat, were cut down and slaughtered to the last man by Clive's Mahrattas. Had Law sent a larger and better commanded force, he would probably have been successful in cutting off Clive's whole detachment. The leader of the deserters was a man named Kelsey, who had been given a commission in the French Army by Dupleix. He was the man who had treacherously tried to kill Clive, when Clive had entered into a parley for the surrender of the enemy. Lawrence ordered him to be hung. This produced lively complaints from Dupleix, who urged the Madras

Council to send Lawrence to Europe to meet the charges of bad faith he, Dupleix, was sending to France against Lawrence. Dupleix was already beginning to see that in Lawrence he had a formidable adversary.

Law, who remained encamped at the western end of the island, now only retained the small post at Pitchandah, north of the Cauvery. At the eastern end of the island he had an important magazine at Coiladdy. d'Auteuil remained at Ootatoor. It was evidently the duty of the two French commanders to fall upon Clive by a concerted movement, while Lawrence was kept in play south of the river. But their whole thoughts were bent on effecting a junction on the island. Lawrence sent a Tanjore force to capture Coiladdy, which was effected on the 26th April. The loss of the supplies stored here soon began to make itself felt in Law's force. The next move was made against d'Auteuil. Events had shown that it was essential not to weaken the force at Samiaveram, so Lawrence sent Dalton across the river with 150 Europeans, 400 Sepoys, 500 Mahratta horse and four guns to attack d'Auteuil. On the evening of the 10th May, Dalton reached a point within two miles of Ootatoor. Before encamping, he sent a party of Europeans and Sepoys to dislodge the enemy from a small village in his front. This was so easily effected that Dalton's men pushed on beyond the village, without orders, and found themselves face to face with d'Auteuil's whole force. After a brief skirmish, in which they lost their officer, they fell back on the village, and held it till Dalton came up. The sun had set, and Dalton worked on d'Auteuil's apprehension by a bold move in the failing light. Keeping his guns in front of the village, with a few men to give the appearance of strength, he sent his whole force of infantry, in two parties, to fall simultaneously on both flanks of d'Auteuil's force. d'Auteuil thought he had to do with the whole of Clive's force, and retreated precipitately to Ootatoor, followed closely by Dalton. Further conflict was prevented by d'Auteuil's cavalry, who had cut in on Dalton's rear, but were driven off by Dalton's Mahrattas. The same night, d'Auteuil evacuated Ootatoor, and fell back eighteen miles on Volcondah, abandoning a great quantity of ammunition and stores.

Dalton's march towards Ootatoor had been seen from the island, but was taken to be part of Clive's force. Law at once crossed the river to attack Samiaveram, and found himself confronted by Clive in a strong position. After some skirmishing, he recrossed the river to Seringham. Two days later, the river rose so as to prevent Dalton rejoining Lawrence. Dalton, with admirable spirit, placed his detachment at Clive's disposal, and offered his own services as a volunteer, to prevent any dispute arising from his superiority of rank. Lawrence, who had already made a lodgment on the island, now ordered Clive to attack Pitchandah. Clive's guns first broke up Law's camp, forcing him and his allies to take refuge about the Jumbakistna temple, and Pitchandah fell after two days' bombardment. The investment of the island was now complete, every part of it being exposed to artillery fire. Lawrence's next move was to cross over to the island at Chucklipolliam, and throw an entrenchment right across the island, east of the Jumbakistna temple, forcing Law and Chunda Sahib to take post at the Seringham temple. Here some delay was necessary in order to get heavy guns from Devicotah. The Europeans with Lawrence on the island were only half the number Law had at his disposal, so a direct attack was out of the

Temple of Seringham.

[To face p. 42.

question; especially as the frequent rising of the river made it impossible for him to depend on co-operation from Clive.

While awaiting the guns from Devicotah, he sent Clive in search of d'Auteuil, on 27th May. Clive found d'Auteuil a few miles south of Volcondah. The English Sepoys, who had outmarched the Europeans, were now so full of ardour that they fell on impetuously, and drove d'Auteuil into the town. The Europeans coming up, carried a gateway by assault, and before morning, on the 29th May, d'Auteuil surrendered with his whole force, consisting of 100 Europeans, 400 Sepoys, 340 horse, three guns and a great quantity of stores, including 800 barrels of powder and 3,000 muskets. Already, before this, Chunda Sahib's people, seeing which way the game was going, and straitened for provisions, had begun to leave him. Chunda Sahib, in despair, entered into negotiations with the Tanjore General for a free passage through his camp, and was treacherously made prisoner. On the 3rd June, Law surrendered, with 35 officers, 785 Europeans, of whom 60 were sick or wounded, 2,000 Sepoys and 45 pieces of artillery. Chunda Sahib was put to death by the Tanjore

General on the same day. And all this had been brought about without a pitched battle. A notable feature in the campaign was the fine military spirit developed among the Sepoys, which had received its first impulse under Clive at Arcot. "It is indeed difficult," says Orme, "to determine whether the English conducted themselves with more ability and spirit, or the French with more irresolution and ignorance, after Major Lawrence and Captain Clive arrived at Trichinopoly."

Dupleix, whom Mill styles "the most audacious contemner of truth that ever engaged in crooked politics," accused Lawrence of having ordered Chunda Sahib's death; and Dupleix's admirers have upheld the unjust accusation so far as to affirm that Lawrence could have saved him if he had chosen. But Lawrence was in no position to dictate to his native allies. The English were auxiliaries, not principals, in the war, and their views had no weight except in the actual business of fighting. Mahomed Ali, the Tanjoreans, the Mysoreans and the Mahrattas, were all equally desirous of getting possession of Chunda Sahib's person to further their own political views, and were equally averse to allowing any of the others to have him in their keeping. When Lawrence offered to settle the dispute by taking charge of the prisoner, the one point on which the confederates agreed was that he should not be made over to the English. Wilks states that Chunda Sahib was put to death at the instigation of Mahomed Ali. Considering the circumstances of the time, his death would appear to have been almost the only solution that would prevent a quarrel among the allies. Not a scrap of evidence has ever been adduced to show that Lawrence was aware such a step was being contemplated, till after the deed was done. It was by Law's advice that Chunda Sahib chose to run any risk rather than surrender himself to the English. The accusation comes with a particularly bad grace from Dupleix, in view of the fact that he had himself resolved on imprisoning Chunda Sahib for life, and at that very time held a firman, secretly obtained from the Nizam, setting aside Chunda Sahib, and placing the Nawabship in the hands of the French.

Law's conduct in retreating to Seringham has been the subject of much adverse criticism, but Lawrence considered it a prudent step at the time. Its effect on Law's native allies was certainly disastrous. But Law cannot be absolved from blame for not opposing Lawrence's march at a sufficient distance from Trichinopoly to prevent the garrison giving him assistance.

No such blow had fallen on the French since they had first entered the field of Indian politics. With great ability, Dupleix reconstructed his plans. The timely arrival of the annual fleet from France brought him reinforcements; by clever intrigues he produced dissension between Mahomed Ali and his native allies; and, by an audacious assumption of authority, claiming the right to act in the name of the Emperor of Delhi, he proclaimed Reza Sahib, Chunda Sahib's son, Nawab of the Carnatic. Two months after Law's surrender, the French inflicted a severe repulse on an English force. The Madras Council, elated by their recent success, resolved to reduce Gingee, an exceptionally strong fortress held by the French, about forty miles from Pondicherry, and seventy-five from Madras. Lawrence, who was at Fort St. David, set out for Madras to dissuade Mr. Saunders from the undertaking. His representations as to the strength of the place, the difficulty of sending supplies to the besieging force, the necessity of settling affairs at Trichinopoly, and the inadequacy of the English forces were not listened to. On July 26th, Major Kinneer, an officer new to the country, arrived before Gingee with 200 Europeans and 2,000 of the Nawab's troops. Dupleix sent an equal force from Pondicherry, under his nephew, M. de Kerjean. Kinneer, finding he had no chance of success against Gingee, marched to meet de Kerjean, who took post at Vicravandi, twenty miles south-east of Gingee, with a river in his front. The English guns, commanded by a French deserter, were badly handled. The attack was repulsed, Kinneer wounded, and many officers and men killed; but Kinneer managed to bring off the rest of his men in good order to Fort St. David. The expedition never had the slightest chance of success. Kinneer died of illness brought on by vexation and disappointment. M. de Kerjean was then sent by Dupleix, with every available man, to blockade Fort St. David. His force amounted to 450 European Infantry, 1,500 Sepoys, fourteen guns, and 500 Native horse. Among the arrivals from Europe, 200 Swiss troops in English pay had reached Madras. Half of them were despatched in open boats to Fort St. David. Lawrence, anticipating what actually happened, strongly urged that the men should not be sent in open boats; but the Council over-ruled him. It was part of the unwritten code that had hitherto governed the acts of the two Companies, while their nations were at peace, that hostilities should not be prosecuted at sea. But Dupleix was not a man to be hampered by scruples in the carrying out of his plans; and, though he would have hesitated to attack a ship, he had no scruples about snapping up defenceless troops in open boats. As the Swiss passed Pondicherry, he intercepted them and made them prisoners. Lawrence, who was ill at the time, at once embarked with the rest of the Swiss for Fort St. David. His force consisted of 400 Europeans, 1,700 Sepoys, and eight or nine field guns, together with three or four thousand of worthless rabble representing the Nawab's troops. De Kerjean, finding he was about to be attacked, broke up his camp and retreated to Bahoor, followed by Lawrence. The next day, the French force moved back to within the bound hedge marking the limits of Pondicherry. According to the curious ethics of the time, Lawrence's instructions forbade his violating French territory, so he contented himself with driving in the French outposts that were outside the boundary hedge, in the hope of bringing on a general action. Seeing that de Kerjean had no intention of leaving his position under the walls of Pondicherry, he formed the project of luring him out of it. Affecting an unwillingness to engage, he fell back precipitately to Bahoor. De Kerjean, against his better judgment, allowed himself to be coerced by Dupleix, under threats of supersession, into following Lawrence, and encamped two miles from Bahoor.

Before daylight, on the 26th August, Lawrence moved out to the attack. Contrary to the usual practice, the advance was led by the Sepoys, the European battalion being kept in reserve. In every action, at that time, the decisive blows were struck by the European troops, and it was essential to ascertain where the French battalion was posted, before the English battalion was too deeply engaged. At the first challenge, the English Sepoys opened fire, but the European battalion continued their advance with shouldered arms. As daylight appeared, the French battalion was discovered, drawn up, with their right resting on a high bank, and their left covered by a small piece of water. The English battalion formed up opposite to them, and advanced under a heavy fire of cannon and small arms. The records of war show that, under such circumstances, one line or the other usually gives way before actual contact; but, at Bahoor, an incident rare in war occurred. The French stood the shock, and the two lines crossed bayonets without flinching. A few minutes of hand to hand fighting ensued, and then the English grenadier company and the two platoons next them broke through the French centre. The whole French line gave way, and fled in confusion. The Nawab's cavalry, instead of pursuing the fugitives, galloped off to plunder the French camp, by which a number of the French were able to escape. M. de Kerjean with fifteen officers and 100 Frenchmen were made prisoners, and a greater number killed, upwards of 100 by the bayonet; eight guns, with all the French ammunition and stores, were captured. Of the English battalion, four officers and seventy-eight men were killed and wounded, mostly by the bayonet, so close and determined was the fighting. In his gratitude to the English, Mahomed Ali, at this time, remitted the ground rent of twelve hundred pagodas a year paid for Fort St. George, and henceforth the East India Company was free of the charge.

In spite of his victory, Lawrence was, for a time, reduced to inaction by the doubtful attitude of the Mysore Durbar and the Mahrattas, under the influence of Dupleix's intrigues. He was engaged in a little fighting and much marching, during which the Mahrattas plundered friend and foe impartially, till a great amount of sickness among his troops forced him to return to Cuddalore.

So little aware were the Directors in London of what was going on in the South of India, that they sent instructions to Lawrence at this time to proceed to Calcutta, to advise about the fortifications there; but Lawrence was too busy to be spared. His whole service in India was confined to the Coromandel coast.

At this time he again sought to relinquish his command. There was frequent discontent among the troops, owing to their pay being constantly in arrears. They were worn out with harassing service, and Lawrence's plans for prosecuting the war were disregarded. He complained that he was not allowed to exercise the powers conferred on him by the Directors, without constant interference. The Governor sent him orders for military movements, without informing him of his plans for prosecuting the war, or paying the slightest attention to his opinions, and made appointments and promotions among the troops without consulting him. In November, he actually relinquished the command, but was prevailed on to resume it after an interval of three weeks.

III.

TRICHINOPOLY

In January, Lawrence was again in the field, engaged in harassing operations, in the neighbourhood of Cuddalore, against the French under M. Maissin, with whom were allied the Mahrattas, who had now definitely declared themselves against Mahomed Ali and the English. On 9th January, he took three guns from the Mahrattas. The French, under M. Maissin, were strongly entrenched in sight of Lawrence's camp at Trivadi, in an unassailable position, and all his efforts to force on a general engagement in the open were unsuccessful. During four months the two armies were in sight of each other, and a number of minor engagements took place between the English and the Mahrattas, in which the want of cavalry on the English side placed Lawrence at some disadvantage. The Mahrattas displayed great energy and gallantry, but the French troops kept themselves in reserve; discouraged, no doubt, by their recent reverses, and also, because it was the design of Dupleix to detain Lawrence and the English force on the coast, while his schemes were working at Trichinopoly. On the 1st April, while bringing up a convoy from Fort St. David, he was attacked by a large Mahratta force supported by a French battalion. Lawrence at once accepted the challenge, and a brisk engagement ensued. The Mahratta leader—Morari Rao's brother—was killed, and the French battalion ran away. Having his convoy to look to, Lawrence was unable to follow up his advantage. Two days later, he threw up a battery and bombarded the French camp, but to no purpose. Unable to bring matters to a decisive issue, Lawrence was relieved from his dilemma by urgent news from Trichinopoly, which caused him to transfer his operations to that neighbourhood.

Mahomed Ali's affairs in Trichinopoly had been going very badly from the time of Law's surrender. In order to secure the Mysore alliance, Mahomed Ali had engaged himself by treaty to surrender Trichinopoly to the Mysore Durbar, without the knowledge of the English, and without the slightest intention of fulfilling his promise. The Tanjore chief had withdrawn, tired of the contest, and Mahomed Ali, without money or supplies, found his only support in Dalton, who had been left at Trichinopoly with 200 Europeans and 1,500 Sepoys after Law's surrender. Before commencing open hostilities, plot after plot was made by the Mysore leader to get rid of Dalton. A plot to assassinate him was detected ; efforts were made to seduce his Sepoys from their allegiance, but without success. Two emissaries, with the Mysore regent's papers in their possession, were given up by a faithful native officer and blown from guns. Then an attempt was made to gain over Poverio, a Neapolitan in the Nawab's service ; but Poverio was true to his salt, and disclosed the plot. The Mysore Regent then put a price on Poverio's head. Lawrence, who was kept informed of all that was going on, proposed that Dalton should seize the Mysore Regent and Morari Rao, by surprise, but the Madras Council disapproved of the project. Mill remarks that the Council would have done well in following Lawrence's advice both in this matter, and in surrendering Trichinopoly to Mysore, according to Mahomed Ali's agreement. " Delicacy would have been less violated in one instance, by following the advice of Lawrence, and prudence would have been more consulted by following it in both." It was at this juncture that Morari Rao, the Mahratta leader, who wanted Trichinopoly for himself, and who had been for some time in correspondence with Dupleix, threw off the mask, and joined Mahomed Ali's enemies. The Mysoreans now began to intercept the entry of provisions into Trichinopoly, and open hostilities were inevitable. Permission was sent from Madras to treat the Mysoreans as enemies. The Mysore army was encamped on the island of Seringham, the scene of Law's surrender. Dalton resolved to beat up their camp. At 10 o'clock at night on the 23rd December, 1752, he marched out, crossed the river, and fell on the Mysore camp. The attack was completely successful, and Dalton regained the city after killing a great number of the enemy, with a loss to himself of only twenty killed and wounded. Being desirous of driving them off the island altogether, he renewed the attack, and seized a small temple which the enemy had occupied. An attack of Mahratta horsemen was repulsed, and all was going well, when a sudden panic seized the men, in consequence of their officer leaving them to communicate with Dalton. They rushed madly to recross the river; the Mahratta horsemen dashed into the fugitives, sabreing right and left, and a disaster was only averted by the steadiness of the remaining troops under Dalton, who had not crossed the river. Two English officers, seventy Europeans, and 300 of the best Sepoys were killed, and Dalton's little force was seriously crippled.

From this date Trichinopoly was closely invested. The Mysore general, with 8,000 men, took up his position at the Fakeer's Tope, south of the city; Dalton, working on his fears, compelled him to retire from it and return to Seringham. But, before this, provisions were running short, and Dalton had been forced to send an express to Lawrence asking for assistance. Lawrence had, for some time, been anxious about the safety of Trichinopoly, but the Council took no action on his representations. On the 19th April he wrote: "If Captain Dalton is to be reinforced, and his situation seems to cry aloud for it, 'tis time to determine something, for the rising of the rivers (and that season is approaching) will put it out of our power to assist him." The intelligence of Trichinopoly's straitened circumstances reached Lawrence at Trivadi, near Cuddalore, at 10 o'clock at night, on the 20th. Leaving 650 men at Trivadi, 150 of whom were Europeans, he marched, at six hours' notice, to Fort St. David to collect supplies. Marching again the next day, he entered Trichinopoly, without fighting, on 6th May, the seventeenth day from the receipt of Dalton's message. Sickness and desertion on the march had considerably reduced the number of his Europeans: 100 of them, unfit for duty, were carried into hospital on the day of his arrival: his whole force, including the original garrison, consisted only of 500 Europeans, 2,000 Sepoys, and 3,000 of the Nawab's horse. His artillery consisted of ten field pieces, and one or two eighteen-pounders. It is worth noting that in taking this sudden decision to march to Dalton's assistance, Lawrence acted without permission of the Madras Council; and it is evident that the long detention of his force near Cuddalore was against his wishes. By his bold march to Trichinopoly, without reference to the Council, Lawrence brought the dispute between Saunders and himself to an issue. The bickerings between them had not ceased, and Saunders had gone so far as to accuse Lawrence of neglecting the Company's interests. The Council not only approved his march, but for the first time disclosed to him their plans, as he had so often solicited. From this time there was perfect accord between Lawrence and the Governor.

Directly Lawrence's withdrawal from Trivadi was known to Dupleix, he despatched M. Astruc with 200 Europeans, 500 Sepoys, and 4 guns to Trichinopoly, without waiting for more definite intelligence of Lawrence's march. All his plans depended on gaining possession of Trichinopoly. Astruc joined the Mysoreans in Seringham the day after Lawrence's arrival at Trichinopoly, and assumed command of the whole force. Astruc was a general of considerable ability. With so great a superiority in numbers, his prospects of success seemed assured. The country in the neighbourhood of Trichinopoly was particularly favourable for his operations. North of the city, the Cauvery River, dividing into two branches, forms the island of Seringham, a stronghold capable alone of containing his whole force. In an irregular three-quarter circle south of the city, and at a distance of between two and four miles, are a number of strong positions known as Elmiseram, French Rocks, Sugarloaf Rock, Golden Rock, Fakeer's Tope, Five Rocks and Weycondah, affording the most favourable ground for an investing force. For thirty years circumstances made Trichinopoly the bone of contention for the contending armies of Southern India. Few spots on earth have been the scene of such continuous fighting as the country for ten miles round Trichinopoly, from 1732 to 1760.

Lawrence was badly off for supplies. His sole chance lay in an active defence, and in being able to gain over the Tanjore Chief, who was still neutral. He was at a great disadvantage through want of cavalry. The Nawab's three thousand horse were quite unable to face the Mysore and Mahratta horsemen led by Hyder Ali and Morari Rao. Giving his troops three days' rest, he marched out to dislodge the French and Mysoreans from Seringham. The engagement was mainly an artillery one. A charge of Rajpoot cavalry was repelled with heavy loss, by the English Sepoys, and Lawrence was forced to return to his camp after the troops had been twenty hours under arms; unsuccessful, but having suffered very slight loss.

The only result of the day's operations had been to show him that, in M. Astruc, he had an abler enemy than he had yet met. He therefore abandoned the idea of dislodging the enemy from Seringham, and devoted himself to procuring supplies. For this purpose, he encamped at the Fakeer's Tope, two and a half miles from the city, so as to prevent a complete investment, and sent parties of Sepoys to procure provisions. In this position he remained five weeks, without being able to bring the French to action, or to procure more provisions than were sufficient for daily consumption. His whole dependence for supplies was on the Chief of Poodoocottah, who was friendly to Mahomed Ali, and whose territory reached to within a few miles of Trichinopoly. He was known in those days by his family title of the Tondiman.

Meanwhile, affairs were going very badly for the English in other parts of the Carnatic. Trivadi, with the force left in it, were captured by the French. A similar mishap occurred at Arcot; every petty chieftain, or soldier of fortune, set up his standard, and ravaged the territories that still gave allegiance to Mahomed Ali. Dupleix, whose whole views were centred on Trichinopoly and the capture of Mahomed Ali, discouraged the Mahrattas from partaking in the general plunder, and prevailed on them to join Astruc, to whom he sent three hundred more Europeans and a thousand Sepoys.

On receipt of these reinforcements, M. Astruc quitted Seringham, crossed the Cauvery, and encamped on the plain to the west of the city, near Weycondah. His force consisted of 450 Europeans, 1,500 well-trained Sepoys, 11,500 Mysore and Mahratta horse, two companies of Topasses (Portuguese native Christians), and 1,200 Sepoys in the Mysore service, and a nondescript, badly armed, undisciplined rabble of 15,000 footmen, more useful to plunder than to fight. Lawrence had at his disposal 500 Europeans, 2,000 Sepoys, of whom 700 were detached from him engaged in collecting and sending in supplies, and 100 of the Nawab's horse. Lawrence's deficiency in cavalry was accentuated by the Mysore and Mahratta horsemen being under two first-rate leaders; the Mysore cavalry under Hyder Ali, who, a few years later, seized the throne of Mysore, and the Mahrattas under Morari Rao. Two miles south-west of the Fakeer's Tope were some rocky hills known as the Five Rocks, where Lawrence maintained a Sepoy guard to keep open the route for the entrance of supplies. Being in a bad state of health he had gone to the city. Through the disobedience of the officer left in command, the guard was withdrawn. Astruc, finding the post undefended, occupied it during the night, advanced his guns and bombarded the English camp. Lawrence maintained his position during the day, and at night withdrew his camp behind a slight eminence nearer the city. Astruc then brought his whole force to the Five Rocks, cutting off Lawrence from the Tondiman's country, and from his absent detachment of 700 Sepoys. Lawrence's position was full of peril. The enemy's position and numbers rendered it impossible to attack them with any prospect of success; Astruc was evidently determined to run no risks; Lawrence's surrender for want of supplies seemed inevitable. There was general despondency in the English camp.

Half a mile from Lawrence's camp, and nearly a mile from Astruc's, was the Golden Rock, where Lawrence maintained a guard of 200 Sepoys. Astruc saw that if he could gain possession of this post he would force back Lawrence into the city, and straiten the investment. At daybreak, on the 26th June, he attacked it with a mixed force of Europeans and Sepoys, and, in spite of a gallant resistance on the part of the defenders, overwhelmed them, killing or taking prisoners the whole of them, before Lawrence could come to their assistance. The French battalion was then brought up behind the rock, the French guns were posted at the base, and opened fire; the whole Mysore army was drawn up about a cannon shot in rear, while the Mahrattas dashed about in small detachments, threatening the flanks and rear of the small English force. Lawrence's position was truly desperate. A number of his Sepoys were absent in the city buying rice; 200 of them had been just destroyed; after providing for the safety of his camp, he could only muster 300 European infantry, 80 artillerymen, and 500 Sepoys. With this force he had advanced to within a short distance of the Golden Rock, before the outpost was overwhelmed. To retreat in face of the numerous horsemen, and pressed by Astruc's Frenchmen, meant probable destruction; yet, to attack a strong position held by such an overwhelming force seemed nothing but sheer madness. Lawrence chose the heroic part. Among his good qualities was his power of inspiring confidence in those who served under him. In a few words he explained the situation to those about him. His officers agreed in the wisdom of attacking, while the men expressed their delight at the opportunity of having "a knock at the Frenchmen" who had kept so long out of reach.

Ordering the grenadier company to assault the rock, Lawrence moved with the rest of his little force round the base of it, to attack the French battalion. Seldom in war has such a sight been seen as this little band of British soldiers moving to the attack, surrounded by many thousands of enemies. Scrambling up the rock, with fixed bayonets and without pulling trigger, cheering as they moved, the unexpected onset of the grenadiers led by Captains Kirk and Kilpatrick, struck the French defenders with panic. Not daring to stand the shock, they fled headlong down the reverse side. Meanwhile, Astruc, behind the rock, not seeing what was happening, had wheeled up his battalion to meet Lawrence, exposing its right flank to the fire of the English grenadiers from the rock, which was increased by some Sepoys who had followed the grenadiers. At this moment, Lawrence drew up his men directly opposite the French front, at twenty yards distance. In spite of M. Astruc's efforts, his men were struck with consternation at seeing themselves attacked by the foe that a few moments before had seemed in their power. Smitten by musketry fire in front and flank, they fell into disorder, which a bayonet charge converted into panic, and they fled from the field, leaving three guns in Lawrence's hands. In vain the Mahrattas strove to retrieve the fortunes of the day. Some of the grenadiers fell under their sabres, while in disorder, taking possession of the guns. But they were soon forced to withdraw, with the loss of many men. Among others, fell Morari Rao's nephew. He had cut down one of the grenadiers, when the man's comrade, who was loading his musket at the time, fired his ramrod through his body. Lawrence sent the corpse back to the Mahrattas in his own palanquin. The French rallied on the Mysore army, and contented themselves with keeping up an ineffective cannonade. For three hours Lawrence remained at the foot of the rock, in the expectation that they would renew the combat. Finding that the French would not advance, he formed his little army into a hollow square, with the captured guns and about seventy prisoners in the centre, and deliberately marched back towards his camp. Hardly had he got clear of the rock, when the whole of the enemy's cavalry, upwards of 10,000 in number, charged furiously down. On several occasions the Mahrattas had succeeded in overwhelming detachments of infantry by dashing in, after first drawing their fire. But the English battalion and sepoys stood firm: not a trigger was pulled. The square was halted and the guns rapidly served, pouring in grape shot into the dense masses, till they broke up and forsook the field, leaving the little band of heroes to march unmolested back to camp, bearing the trophies of victory. No finer feat of arms was ever performed.

The first result of this victory was to produce dissensions between the French and their allies. M. Astruc made over his command to M. Brenier, and repaired to Pondicherry. Lawrence got in fifty days' provisions, and leaving Dalton with a small garrison, marched towards Tanjore, thirty miles distant. His object in view was to induce the Tanjore Chief to furnish him with cavalry, and to meet a reinforcement on its way from the coast.

Brenier closely invested the City, and, could he but have summoned resolution to assault it, would probably have taken it. But Dalton's vigilance, together with occasional sorties, prevented any such attempt.

Lawrence, meanwhile, had gained over the Tanjore Chief, who furnished him with 3,000 horse, and 2,000 matchlock men. He also received a reinforcement of 170 Europeans and 300 Sepoys from Fort St. David. With his force thus increased, Lawrence arrived within ten miles of Trichinopoly. Brenier determined to intercept him, and, with this purpose, occupied the whole of the strong positions south of the City from Weycondah to Elmiseram. The centre of the whole position, the Golden and Sugarloaf Rocks, about half a mile apart, was strongly held by the French infantry and artillery. On the 9th August, Lawrence resumed his advance. Encumbered with thousands of bullocks it appeared impossible for him to force a passage. He had, however, the advantage of an exact knowledge of the disposition of Brenier's forces communicated to him by Dalton. The key of the French position was the Golden Rock. Lawrence formed up his men as if he intended to attack the Sugar loaf Rock. Brenier fell into the trap, and denuded the Golden Rock to strengthen the point apparently threatened. Lawrence thereupon detached his grenadier company, with 800 Sepoys, to seize the Golden Rock; a movement not perceived by the French commander till too late to prevent it. Brenier dispatched 300 Europeans to strengthen the small party he had left at the Golden Rock, and a thousand cavalry to hamper the English infantry on their way. But the grenadiers did not permit themselves to be delayed. Without halting, they kept up a rolling fire on the horsemen, who refrained from closing, till, reaching the Golden Rock, they drove the enemy down and planted their colours on the top, before the infantry detached by Brenier could reach the spot. Instead of making an effort to recover the position, this party then took post on some high ground between the two rocks, and opened a galling fire with four guns upon the Golden Rock. Brenier, instead of moving his main body to support his detachment, remained halted near the Sugarloaf Rock in a state of indecision, while Lawrence moved his whole force, convoy and all, to the Golden Rock.

An artillery duel ensued in which the English battalion suffered some loss. At this juncture, Dalton issued from the City with two field pieces and his detachment, in rear of the enemy's cavalry, who broke up and galloped off. Seeing Brenier's main body still stationary, Lawrence sent the grenadier company and 200 Europeans, with 300 Sepoys, against the French detachment. The officer ordered for the attack sent back word that he could not proceed without cannon. Lawrence galloped up and took command, sending back the officer to the main body. They were received with a heavy fire, which caused some loss, and killed Captain Kirk of the grenadiers. Captain Kilpatrick put himself at the head of the grenadiers, desiring them, if they loved their Captain, to follow him and avenge his death. "These things on the spot have generally a very great effect, when delivered from a person whose spirit and courage is known," as Lawrence afterwards wrote, describing the affair. "The fellows, roused in an instant, swore, after their manner, they would follow him to hell," and avenge Kirk's death. The French broke, without awaiting the shock, and ran off to Weycondah, galled by Dalton's guns, leaving three field pieces in Lawrence's hands. Brenier, when it was now too late, moved up his main body; but his men, seeing Lawrence's whole force in motion, lost heart, and, without waiting to exchange shots, ran off in great confusion to the Five Rocks, exposed to a severe cannonade from the English guns at the Golden Rock. The Tanjore horse, who might have destroyed them, refused to pursue, and so the battle ended. Lawrence, collecting his force, marched into the city with his convoy and the captured guns. Of the French, about one hundred Europeans were killed and wounded; of the English, about forty; principally by artillery fire.

In the course of the action Lawrence's palanquin bearers had straggled from the line of march, and were snapped up by the Mahrattas. Lawrence sent to redeem it, but before this could be done, the French got hold of it, and sent it to Pondicherry, where Dupleix had it paraded through the streets as a token of Lawrence's defeat and death.

During Lawrence's absence, Dalton had been closely blockaded in Trichinopoly. On one occasion a French officer, feigning himself to be a deserter, gained access to the town, in order to communicate the weak places of the defence to Brenier, and head an outbreak of the French prisoners. He was detected, and hanged after Lawrence's return.

A fortnight later, Lawrence moved out against Weycondah, where Brenier had concentrated his force and thrown up entrenchments. The French abandoned the position without resistance, and took post at Mootachellinoor on the Cauvery, leaving a gun and some baggage in Lawrence's hands. Here Brenier was joined by a strong reinforcement under M. Astruc, consisting of 400 Europeans, 2,000 Sepoys, six guns, and 3,000 Mahratta cavalry, together with a great number of irregular infantry. The English were again as much outnumbered as they had been at any time during the war. Astruc again assumed command. He reoccupied the positions of the Five Rocks and the Golden and Sugarloaf Rocks, entrenched himself, and recommenced the blockade, instead of making use of his great superiority of force to bring matters to a conclusion. Lawrence moved out into the open plain, south-east of the French Rock, to give a hand to the convoys coming in from

Tanjore, while he awaited a reinforcement that was on its way to him. For eighteen days the two armies remained thus encamped, at about two miles distance from each other, on an open plain, without a bush on it between them; so that, with a glass, each could see what was going on in the other's camp. The difference in *morale* between the two armies may be gathered from the fact that the English were encamped on the open plain, while the superior force of the French had their front covered by entrenchments. On the night of the 18th September, Lawrence seized a small eminence between the camps, brought an 18-pounder out of the city, and opened fire with it on the French camp. The French detached a party against the 18-pounder. A skirmish ensued, under cover of which the expected reinforcements, consisting of 237 Europeans and 300 Sepoys, under Captain Ridge, joined him without molestation. With Ridge also came Captain Caillaud, who was destined in time to succeed Lawrence, and who, among other performances, outwitted d'Auteuil on this very ground four years later.

Having nothing to gain by further delay, Lawrence at once took the offensive. His troops were in high spirits, but he had only three days' provisions, so action was necessary. Depositing his tents in the city, he drew up his little army at the Fakeer's Tope, at daybreak on the 20th, and offered battle. M. Astruc not accepting the challenge, Lawrence sent for his tents, and pitched camp, with the view of disarming suspicion. The cannonade from the 18-pounder was maintained "that they might think we had no other view than that of disturbing them in their camp with our shot. This lulled them into a security." After dark, the tents were packed up and sent back to the city, and preparations made to attack. Lawrence's force consisted of 600 European infantry, in three divisions, 100 European artillerymen with six guns, 2,000 Sepoys, and the Tanjorine cavalry and matchlockmen. At four in the morning of the 21st September, the army started. The European infantry marching in three divisions in column, the guns were disposed on either flank, and the Sepoys followed in two lines in rear of the guns; the Tanjorine cavalry in rear of the whole.

The object of first attack was the Golden Rock, on which Astruc had posted 100 Europeans, 600 Sepoys, and two guns, with two companies of Topasses. It was a bright moonlight night, but clouds obscured the moon as the force moved out; so that they arrived within pistol shot of the rock before they were discovered. Pouring in a volley, they rushed to the assault with such ardour that the enemy fled precipitately, without even waiting to fire their two cannon, which were ready loaded with grape. Without waiting longer than was necessary to disable the guns, the force advanced again, the Europeans in line, with the Sepoys, in short echelon, on either flank. The French had entrenched the front of their camp, but the adjoining native camp was not entrenched. Lawrence's plan was to penetrate the native camp and, through it, to attack the French camp, thus turning the entrenchment, while the Tanjore horse, with some matchlockmen, were directed to move against the French front, and threaten an attack in that quarter. With drums beating, portfires lighted, and the Sepoys' native instruments in full blast, the British force advanced with loud cheers into the Mysore camp, spreading consternation everywhere. Nine French guns were brought into action, but, with such ill effect in the dark, that they did harm mostly to their native allies. The Sepoys kept up a smart fire, while the Europeans marched with fixed bayonets and shouldered arms. As day was breaking, the Mysore camp was cleared, and the French battalion was discovered drawn up in line, with a large body of Sepoys on their left flank, while another large body, who had been directed to cover their right flank, had, instead, taken post on the Sugarloaf Rock. Reforming their disordered lines as they advanced, and reserving their fire, the English infantry were received with a volley at twenty paces, which caused some loss; Captain Kilpatrick, leading the grenadiers on the right of the European battalion, falling desperately wounded. But the Sepoys on the left of the French line broke and fled under the fire of the English Sepoys. Caillaud, who had taken Kilpatrick's place, seized the opportunity, and wheeled up the right division of the European battalion on the uncovered left flank of the French battalion, poured in a heavy fire and charged with the bayonet, rolling them up on their centre; while the remainder of the English battalion fell upon them in front. The French fell back in disorder, Astruc doing his best to rally them. But the English grenadiers were on them again before they could re-form; in a moment the whole French force dissolved and fled in complete disorder, dispersing in every direction. The overthrow of the French battalion was completed in ten or twelve minutes. The English Sepoys on the left, who had taken no part in the engagement so far, pushed on to the Sugarloaf Rock, which they carried, completely defeating and dispersing the French Sepoys posted there.

The whole affair scarcely lasted two hours. On beholding the defeat of the French, their native allies dispersed in flight. The whole plain was covered with the flying enemy, who were computed at 30,000 footmen and 16,000 horse. In wild confusion, the great mass of fugitives, mingled with elephants, camels and bullocks, fled, as they best could, for Mootachellinoor, not stopping till they had crossed the Cauvery on to the island of Seringham. The Tanjore horse, as usual, instead of pursuing, amused themselves with plundering the French camp. M. Astruc, with nine officers, and 100 Frenchmen, eleven pieces of cannon and all the tents, baggage, and ammunition of the French camp, remained in the hands of the victors. Dalton, sallying out from the city, took twenty-one French prisoners, sixty-five more were found straggling in Tanjore territory, and a number were knocked on the head by the country people, wandering in the woods: 200 of them were killed or wounded in the engagement, and the Mahratta horse alone saved the French European infantry from total destruction. A thousand of the French native allies were killed and wounded. Of the English, six officers and seventy men were killed or wounded, among the latter being Lawrence himself. Kilpatrick, in spite of being shot through the body, and receiving several sabre wounds from Mahratta horsemen as he lay on the ground, survived to fight again. The action was decided entirely by the infantry: the English guns were never engaged, while the French guns were so badly served that they only inflicted damage on their own allies.

Lawrence followed up his victory by laying siege to Weycondah, the same evening. Early on the 23rd, before the breach was ready for assault, the English Sepoys, seeing some of the garrison escaping, broke away from their officers, and tried to mount the breach. Finding this impracticable, they made for the gateway. A sergeant of Sepoys, "a resolute Englishman," whose name has not been preserved, clambered up by the carved work, and planted the colours of his company on the parapet. He was quickly joined by some of his men; the gate was opened, and those outside rushed in with such fury, with the bayonet, that the garrison flung down their arms and surrendered. Then Lawrence, after sweeping a large quantity of supplies into the city, where he left a small garrison, marched for Tanjore, where his presence was needed to counteract the intrigues of Dupleix. In spite of his efforts, heavy bribes from Pondicherry succeeded in procuring the removal of the only efficient Tanjore commander, while threats of a Mahratta invasion practically reduced the timid ruler of Tanjore to neutrality again. In November, a French reinforcement of 300 Europeans and 1,200 Sepoys, under M. Maissin reached Seringham. Their arrival was carefully kept secret, and everything was done to put the Trichinopoly garrison off their guard. At three o'clock in the morning of the 28th November, a determined attempt was made to surprise Trichinopoly. A chosen body of 600 Frenchmen, led by an English deserter, crossed the ditch, and seized a detached battery, without alarming the main garrison. Nothing more was needed for success but to blow in a small side gate, for which all preparations had been made. Elated by their first success, the French disobeyed their orders, and commenced firing. The alarm was given. Kilpatrick, who was in command, was still confined to his bed by his wounds, but his orders to his subaltern, Lieutenant Harrison, were coolly obeyed. The picquet and reserve hastened to the rampart and opened fire. By great good fortune, the guide and both powder bearers were killed ; the French, between the outer and inner walls, unable to advance or retreat, and without a guide, were exposed to a merciless fire, and, as soon as daylight permitted, they were glad to surrender. A number attempted the desperate expedient of leaping down into the ditch, when they found the enterprise had failed. Few escaped without serious injury ; but all were carried off by their associates who had remained outside. Eight officers and 364 men were taken prisoners, one officer and twenty-four men killed, and a number wounded. Thus, "French petulance," as Lawrence styled it, saved Trichinopoly from the greatest risk it had run during the war.

The acute phase of the struggle was at an end. Lawrence could defeat the French, but he could not drive them away, backed up as they were by some of the best cavalry in Southern India, a force in which he was lamentably deficient. Dupleix, now at the end of his resources, attempted to come to an arrangement with the English, hoping to win by diplomacy what he had failed to win by force. In January, 1754, commissioners from both sides met at the Dutch settlement at Sadras; but their views were quickly found to be irreconcilable. On the English side the commissioners laid down, as a basis of negotiation, that Mahomed Ali should be recognised as Nawab of the Carnatic, and that the Tanjore Chief should be guaranteed in the peaceable possession of his kingdom. The French terms were based on the recognition of Salabut Jung as Soobadar of the Deccan, and the rejection of the claims of Mahomed Ali. They also produced Sunnuds from Salabut Jung, appointing Dupleix commander in all the countries south of the River Kistna, and granting him Arcot and Trichinopoly. The whole was capped by a Firman from Delhi confirming the grants made by Salabut Jung. The English held this latter document to be a forgery, as it probably was. Apart from the Moghul Firman, which, after all, had only an academic value, the position of the English in Southern India would have become untenable had they agreed to the French demands; so the conference was broken up in eleven days from its commencement. Dupleix had, in fact, demanded the specific assent of the English to what they had all along been contending against.

At the same time, negotiations were opened with the English, by the Mysore Regent, for the possession of Trichinopoly. The Madras Council wished Lawrence to conduct the negotiations: he excused himself on the plea of health, but really because he disapproved of the conditions. He had all along held the opinion that Mahomed Ali should be forced to observe his promise to deliver Trichinopoly to Mysore, and he did not cease to express his regret "that the attempt had been made to keep Trichinopoly after promising to cede it." The Madras Council had all along held a different opinion. They now made the absurd proposal that Trichinopoly should be held by the English till the other articles of the proposed treaty with Mysore were carried out; and that a certain proportion of Mysore troops should be introduced into the garrison. Lawrence bluntly wrote to them: "Give me leave to tell you the proposal is absurd and impracticable." The negotiation, after dragging on for a long time, came to nothing.

While these negotiations were going on, Lawrence was encamped at Trichinopoly, confronting the French Force in Seringham, under M. de Mainville. The country for a great distance round had been denuded of supplies of every kind by the warfare of the two previous years, and Lawrence was dependent for provisions on Tanjore. Supplies were brought in by the Tanjore merchants to Tricatopoly, eighteen miles east of Trichinopoly, whence they were escorted in by detachments from Lawrence's camp. The duty was one of great fatigue and risk to the small force Lawrence had with him, encumbered as he was with a great number of French prisoners. There were sufficient English troops to spare to have strengthened his force, but the Council chose to keep them on the coast. In the middle of February, a more important convoy than usual was on its way from Tricatopoly. Lawrence sent out a detachment of 230 Europeans, about 500 Sepoys, and 4 guns, under Captain Grenville, to bring it in.* Grenville had orders to keep his force together, and, if attacked, to take up a position and defend himself, till Lawrence could come to his relief. De Mainville had notice of the convoy, and detached 400 Europeans, 6,000 Sepoys, and 7 guns with 8,000 Mahratta horse, to intercept it. On the morning of the 15th February, Grenville had reached a point between Elmiseram and the river when he was attacked. Disregarding his orders, he had distributed his men on both sides of the convoy along its whole length. On seeing the enemy, he made no attempt to get his men together or to take up a position, and the whole detachment was overwhelmed by the Mahrattas, almost without striking a blow. The French troops only came up in time to save the lives of some of them. Men, guns, supplies, and £7,000 in money were lost, and Grenville paid for his error with his life. Here also Lawrence lost

* These are the numbers given in Lawrence's letter written ten days after the event. In his later narrative he adopts the numbers given by Orme—viz., 180 Europeans and 800 Sepoys.

that splendid company of grenadiers that he had formed with such care, and so often led to victory. Though it is nowhere mentioned, there can be little doubt that it was the company he made his own. Of the 230 Europeans lost to him that day, 138 were prisoners, only thirty-eight of them being taken unwounded. Of the eight officers present, four were killed and three wounded.

This disaster reduced Lawrence to great straits. He was no longer able to send parties to bring in convoys from Tanjore, and was obliged to depend on the Tondiman's country for precarious supplies. He was oppressed by serious illness, and despaired of ultimate success, with the insufficient means at his disposal. For the escorting of his small convoys he was principally dependent on a gallant native soldier, Mahomed Yusuf, of Nellore. This man had first entered the Company's service, under Clive, at the beginning of 1751, at the head of a small body of men raised by himself. Lawrence describes him as "an excellent partisan . . . brave and resolute, but cool and wary in action. He was never sparing of himself . . . a born soldier, and better of his colour I never saw in the country. He always prevents my asking, by offering himself for everything, and executes what he goes about as well and as briskly as he attempts it." On Lawrence's recommendation, Mahomed Yusuf was, at this time, granted a commission as commandant of all the Sepoys in the Company's service.

All Lawrence's communications with native authorities were carried on through his interpreter, a Brahmin named Poniapa, whose position, necessarily, made him acquainted with important secrets. Poniapa entered into a secret correspondence with the Mysore Regent, whom he induced to demand that he, Poniapa, should be sent by Lawrence to receive proposals for the termination of the war. Lawrence sent him, and he returned with a plausible report; having really engaged with the Regent to betray the English, whose difficulties in procuring supplies he revealed. As a first step, he informed the Regent that it was necessary to get rid of Mahomed Yusuf. For this purpose he arranged that an incriminating letter from the Mysore Regent, addressed to Mahomed Yusuf, should be dropped in the English camp. This was done, and the letter brought to Lawrence, as had been intended, and read to him by Poniapa. Lawrence was completely deceived, and Mahomed Yusuf was at once imprisoned. His fate would have been sealed, had not, by good fortune, the man who dropped the letter been discovered. He was confronted with Poniapa, and the Brahmin was forced to confess the truth. As a fitting punishment, Poniapa was blown from a gun, by sanction of the Madras Council, and Mahomed Yusuf exonerated. But the narrowness of his escape, and the danger of serving people who were at the mercy of interpreters, is said to have made an impression on Mahomed Yusuf that was never effaced from his mind, and bore evil fruit eight years later.

On 12th May, Lawrence detached a party under Captain Caillaud, consisting of 120 men with 500 Sepoys and 2 guns, to escort in a convoy coming from the Tondiman's country. De Mainville had intelligence of the convoy, and sent a detachment of troops with some Mysore horse and four guns to intercept it at the point where Caillaud was to meet it. The Mahrattas, fortunately, were absent; having quarrelled with the Mysoreans the day before. Caillaud left camp at four in the morning, with Mahomed Yusuf reconnoitring in front. Suddenly, Mahomed Yusuf's horse neighed, and was answered by many others. Riding to the top of a bank, Mahomed Yusuf was received with an ill-directed volley which disclosed the position of the ambush. So far as could be made out in the dark, the French were posted under cover of a bank. Caillaud sent parties against both flanks at once, who drove them from their cover with the loss of some men and a tumbril of ammunition. He then sent off a messenger to turn the convoy back, and waited for daylight. Directly the firing was heard in camp Captain Polier* marched out to join Caillaud; bringing up their joint force to 360 Europeans, 1,500 Sepoys, and 11 English troopers with 5 guns. Lawrence was ill, in the city, at the time; too ill to move. He had himself carried to the ramparts, whence he viewed the combat with much anxiety. French reinforcements had also come up, bringing up their force to 700 Europeans, 50 dragoons, 5,000 Sepoys, 10,000 Mysore horse and 7 guns. Polier commenced

* He was a Swiss officer, and his real name was Polier de Bottens. He was killed at the beginning of the siege of Madras, December, 1758.

his retreat in the face of this overwhelming force, and, for a mile, his party moved with great steadiness, harassed by French cannon and musketry fire, till they were able to take post under cover of a bank. Two of the guns had been disabled, but were still brought along, and Polier himself was wounded, and obliged to make over the command to Caillaud. Caillaud drew up his Europeans to face the advancing French battalion, and opened a heavy fire of grape on them from two guns; while the Sepoys were drawn up, *en potence*, protecting the left flank and rear of the Europeans against the Mysore cavalry. So effectively were the guns served that the French battalion halted, wavered and began to retreat. Caillaud seized the moment to advance and fire a volley, which threw the French into complete disorder. In spite of the efforts of their officers they fell back; the example was followed by their Sepoys and Mysore allies, and Caillaud resumed his march without further molestation. Six out of the nine officers present were wounded; fifty-five soldiers and one hundred and fifty Sepoys were killed and wounded.

The French, disheartened by their constant

failures against Trichinopoly, now adopted the expedient of ravaging the territories of the Tondiman, and of Tanjore, whence Lawrence drew the supplies that enabled him to maintain his position. They were able to do little damage beyond destroying the dam of the Cauvery river, on which much of the prosperity of Tanjore depended ; but a Tanjore force of 1,500 men was overwhelmed by Morari Rao. Lawrence, leaving a sufficient garrison in Trichinopoly, and calling in all his outposts, marched for Tanjore, where he procured the reinstatement of the Tanjore commander, who had been displaced through the intrigues of Dupleix. Here he remained some weeks, and received a reinforcement of Europeans and Sepoys, while waiting for the co-operation of the Tanjore army, which was as dilatory in its movements as native armies always were.

On the 16th August, Lawrence and his allies encamped six miles west of Elmiseram. Lawrence's force now consisted of 1,000 European infantry, 200 Topasses, 3,000 Sepoys, and 14 field guns. The Tanjore force mustered 2,500 cavalry, 3,000 infantry, and some guns. M. de Mainville, with the French force, had all this time been hovering round Trichinopoly without making any serious attack. On the 16th August, orders from Pondicherry constrained him to relinquish the command to M. Maissin. Maissin moved from the Five Rocks to intercept Lawrence. His force consisted of 900 European infantry, 400 Topasses, a number of Sepoys, 8 guns, and 10,000 Mysore horse under Hyder Ali. Marching on the 17th, Lawrence was able to seize a deep watercourse and high bank between French Rock and Elmiseram, which Maissin had designedly failed to occupy. In concert with Hyder Ali, he had arranged to draw the English force towards Five Rocks, when Hyder Ali was to seize a favourable opportunity to fall on the baggage and convoy. The plan nearly succeeded.

Lawrence, seeing the French drawn up in order of battle on his left, at once accepted the challenge, and advanced in two lines. A hot cannonade ensued, in which the French suffered a good deal, and, as the opposing lines were on the point of commencing musketry fire, the French went about, and retreated in good order towards Five Rocks. Lawrence was preparing to follow, when he received news of Hyder Ali's attack on his rear. In his impatience, Hyder Ali had moved too soon. Leaving some of his cavalry to keep the Tanjore horse in play, he had galloped round French Rock, and was driven off, after causing some confusion, carrying off thirty-five carts laden with arms, ammunition and baggage. A separate attack made by the French, from the island of Seringham, was met by a sortie from Trichinopoly under Kilpatrick, who drove them back to the island without loss to himself. Maissin, who had orders not to risk a general engagement, offered no further opposition, and Lawrence entered Trichinopoly, with the loss of one officer and fifteen men. The French had a hundred Europeans killed and wounded.

Three days later, Lawrence moved out to the Fakeer's Tope, in the hope of provoking an engagement: the French set fire to their camp, and drew off to Mootachellinoor, leaving the road open for Lawrence's supplies to come in. The same evening the French fortified post at Elmiseram was invested by the Tanjore troops, and surrendered two days later. Finding the French were entrenched at Mootachellinoor, Lawrence moved to Warriore. So little confidence had the French in themselves that, in spite of the strength of their position which was covered by an inundation from the Cauvery on both flanks, they abandoned the entrenchment by night, and retreated across the river to Seringham.

Further operations were suspended on account of the rainy season. In October, news was received of a truce, preparatory to a definite peace having been established between the French and English Companies, and of the recall of Dupleix. At the same time, Lawrence received notice of the grant to him of a sword of honour, worth £750, by the Court of Directors.

The services Lawrence rendered his country, in 1752 and 1753, cannot be over-estimated. In 1751, French power in India was at its zenith. A French Nizam ruled at Hyderabad, and a French Nawab was predominant in the Carnatic. From the Nerbudda to Cape Comorin the whole country was practically under French domination. Had Dupleix triumphed at Trichinopoly, the expulsion of the English from Madras and Fort St. David would have quickly followed. Lawrence's victories turned the scale, and brought about the withdrawal of Dupleix, in whom France lost the services of the ablest statesman she ever sent to India. Within seven years of Dupleix's departure, the fortunes of France in India were irretrievably ruined. Again and again Dupleix had assured the French Government that the British were on the brink of destruction; that one effort more only was required, and all the wealth of India would be in their grasp. The repeated defeats and disappointments destroyed Dupleix's credit in France, and he was recalled to end his days in disgrace and ruin, just one month before the first Royal regiment from England landed in India. M. Cultru, in his study of Dupleix, states that it was the defeat of Law in 1752 that had a decisive effect on Dupleix's career, by destroying his credit in France. All his previous services were at once forgotten. But it may be doubted if the death of Chunda Sahib was not more disastrous to Dupleix's policy, than Law's surrender was to French arms. Chunda Sahib's ability made him a better candidate for the Nawabship than Mahomed Ali, and, after his death, Dupleix failed to find any decent claimant to the Carnatic throne, under cover of whose name he could prosecute his schemes of aggrandisement, till he was prepared to assume

JOSEPH-FRANÇOIS, MARQUIS DUPLEIX,

Commandeur de l'Ordre Royal et Milit.^e de St Louis,
Commandant Général des Etablisemens françois dans
l'Inde, Gouv.^r pour le Roy des Ville et fort de Pondichery;
né à Landrecy en 1697; mort à Paris le 11 9bre 1763.

the government himself. In the following year, the French with their Mysore and Mahratta allies were far stronger in the field than the English, and had every prospect of regaining the prestige they had lost by Law's defeat.

The East India Directors had at last realised that if they wished to preserve their trade they must be prepared, at all times, to fight for it. The territorial expansion that followed in due course of time was forced upon them in their own defence. At the end of 1754, a treaty of peace* was signed between the English and French Companies, which gave both nations in India a short breathing time, before the outbreak of the Seven Years' War.

* A curious feature about the treaty was that it did not fully provide for the restoration of prisoners of war. It provided only for a mutual exchange, man for man. No less than 670 French prisoners were in Trichinopoly at the time. Of these some died and some—Swiss and Germans—entered the English service: but when war broke out again in April, 1757, there were still 500 French prisoners in Trichinopoly. These prisoners were not exchanged till May, 1759. No sooner had they rejoined the French army, under Lally, than they raised a mutiny, and some sixty of them marched off in a body to join the English.

IV.

DEFENCE OF MADRAS

WITH the advent of the 39th Regiment in India, Lawrence received notice that the King had bestowed on him the commission of a Lieutenant-Colonel in the East Indies; but this did not save him from the loss of the chief command of troops in the field. Though he held the appointment of Commander-in-Chief under the Company, the command of the Royal troops was dependent on seniority, and Adlercron, who commanded the 39th, was senior to Lawrence by date of commission. Lawrence refused to serve under Adlercron, and retained only his command of the Company's troops. For two years his work was chiefly administrative. When the news came, in 1756, of the capture of Calcutta by Sooraj-ud Dowla, and preparations for an expedition for its recapture were made, Adlercron was set aside by general consent, owing to his want of experience of the country, and to the independence of his position towards the Company's officials. Ill-health prevented Lawrence from taking the command, and Clive was selected.

In April, 1757, the French took the field again, consequent on the breaking out of the Seven Years' War in Europe. Their first move was an attempt to capture Trichinopoly.

On the 12th May, d'Auteuil, with 1,150 Europeans and 3,000 Sepoys, occupied Seringham, and, three days later, commenced to bombard the city. Caillaud, who held the command at Trichinopoly, was away besieging Madura, which had been seized by Mahfoos Khan. Trichinopoly was held only by 165 Europeans and 700 Sepoys under Captain Joseph Smith. Smith was embarrassed by the presence of 500 French prisoners, whose release was one of d'Auteuil's objects. For ten days the garrison was harassed by bombardment and threatened assaults, when the news of Caillaud's approach caused d'Auteuil to draw off, and dispose his army to intercept him, by occupying the old positions at the Five Rocks, Fakeer's Tope, &c. Caillaud, with 120 Europeans and 1,200 Sepoys, marching without artillery, tents or baggage, had arrived within twelve miles of the city when he received Smith's messengers telling him of the disposal of d'Auteuil's forces. At the same time he detected the presence of d'Auteuil's spies in his camp. Affecting not to notice them, while keeping them under surveillance, he marched, in the evening, as if to pass between the Five Rocks and the Sugarloaf Rock. After satisfying himself that the spies had gone off to carry the news to d'Auteuil, he changed the direction of his march, and striking eastward, emerged from the woods opposite Elmiseram. The whole plain was at this time a deep swamp, under rice cultivation. d'Auteuil, believing it to be impassable, had not even stationed a guard here. After seven hours of terrible fatigue, but without a single shot being fired, Caillaud reached Chucklipolliam on the Cauvery. A salute of twenty-one guns, at daybreak, announced to d'Auteuil that he had been outwitted. He at once broke up his camp and marched for Pondicherry.

Before this, the Council had sent Adlercron, with what troops the Presidency could furnish, to Smith's relief. Adlercron's movements were so slow that he took six days to accomplish thirty miles, and was still at Ootramaloor when the news of Caillaud's arrival in Trichinopoly reached him. He then marched on Wandiwash, and captured the Pettah, but seeing no chance of success against the fort, before the arrival of the French, who were now advancing, he fell back on Ootramaloor, to await instructions. The Council, distrustful of Adlercron, ordered him to return to Madras. A French force, under Saubinet, had reached Wandiwash before Adlercron commenced his march for Madras, and occupied Ootramaloor a few hours after he left it. Adlercron, without informing the Council, or taking any steps to oppose the French, continued his march to Madras. The French at once advanced on Conjeveram, which they burned; but they failed to take the Pagoda, which was stoutly held by Sergeant Lambertson and two companies of Sepoys. The Council, sensible of their mistake in leaving the fertile country of the Paliar valley open to the French, ordered Adlercron to take the field again.

During his three years in India, Adlercron was a continual source of embarrassment to the Council. He was a dull, incompetent man, puffed up with a sense of his own importance in commanding the King's troops, The instructions he had been furnished with, before leaving England, had not been submitted to the Directors, and were of such a nature as to ensure a clash of authority. The Council in Madras, annoyed at being deprived, by an accident, of the services of an experienced officer like Lawrence, were dismayed at the prospect of the operations in the field being directed by Adlercron. For three years their efforts were directed to getting the use of Adlercron's troops without Adlercron. Adlercron, on his side, was determined that, unless he himself had the command, his troops should not be employed. The services of the 250 men of the 39th, who helped to recover Calcutta, were only secured on the understanding that they were to act as Marines under the Admiral. Adlercron's incompetence and obstructiveness, combined with his seniority of rank, threatened to paralyse all military operations in India. At a time when the presence of every British soldier was worth his weight in gold, the Company had been forced to move the Crown to recall the 39th Regiment, merely to get rid of Adlercron. But a year and a half were to elapse before the representations of the Madras Council bore fruit. The brief experience they had now had of Adlercron in the field, only served to increase their distrust of his capacity for command. In this dilemma, Lawrence, who had hitherto refused to serve under Adlercron, now offered to accompany him as a volunteer. Making his way, by sea, to Fort St. David, he took a hundred men from the garrison there, landed at Sadras, and joined Adlercron near Chingleput. The army marched for Ootramaloor, where it remained for forty days, within a few hours' march of the French, without a shot being fired. In a letter written by Adlercron at this time, dated Ootramaloor 29th June, 1757, he says: "What increases my confidence of success is that I am assisted with Colonel Lawrence, who is not only deservedly esteemed for his military capacity, but has a thorough knowledge of the situation of the country. This gentleman is in such favour with the Company's managers that, in order he might have command of the army, the Committee had the assurance to propose my staying at Fort St. George to assist them in their Councils, which they have always hitherto kept private from me." It apparently never occurred to Adlercron that Lawrence had waived his objections to serving under him, in order to be at hand to keep him out of scrapes.

It was found impossible to bring the French to action, except at a great disadvantage; there was much sickness among the troops, so, by Lawrence's advice, the army fell back on Conjeveram at the end of July. Neither side was in a position to undertake active operations. At the end of the year, the 39th were ordered to embark for England, and Lawrence once more became the senior officer in India. Several officers and 350 men of the 39th transferred their services to the Company.

For the first two years of the war, the English forces in Madras were reduced to act on the defensive. Every available man who could be spared had been sent to Bengal with Clive. Fortunately, the French did not take all the advantage that was open to them, and only indulged in secondary operations, while awaiting the large armaments that were on their way from France. In the meantime, Bussy seized the English factories in the Northern Circars. On some reinforcements reaching Pondicherry, the French over-ran the Carnatic, snapping up all the strongholds in native hands, and took Chittapet from the English.

At the end of April, 1758, Count Lally arrived at Pondicherry with a powerful fleet commanded by d'Aché, field guns and troops, and plenary powers over the whole of the French troops and possessions in India. The English, in this hour of weakness, had been forced to retire from all their conquests in Southern India. Trichinopoly, Arcot, Chingleput and Conjeveram alone remained to them, besides Madras, Fort St. David and Cuddalore on the coast. Within five weeks of Lally's arrival, Cuddalore and Fort St. David were captured, and Lally determined to march on Madras. But d'Aché refused to support him with the fleet, and money was wanting. To remedy this evil, Lally determined to attack Tanjore. He laid siege to the place, but, at the end of three weeks, was forced to relinquish the enterprise and return to Pondicherry. D'Aché, too, was worsted in an encounter with Pocock, off Tranquebar, and left the coast Before doing so he seized a Dutch ship. though France and Holland were at peace, and thus obtained money for Lally to equip his army.

On the 12th December, Lally appeared before Madras and occupied the town. Lawrence, who had taken post at St. Thomas's Mount, fell back before the French advance. On his entering the fort the command of the troops devolved on the Council, according to the practice of the time under the Company's sway. The Council committed the defence of the fort to the Governor, Mr. Pigot, recommending him to consult Lawrence on all occasions, and, on extraordinary emergencies, to assemble a council of the superior officers of the garrison. The defence practically devolved on Lawrence, who had, at the moment, under him, an exceptionally able body of officers formed by himself in the past ten years. Three of his best officers remained outside Fort St. George: Caillaud and Preston to carry on a partisan warfare against the French rear, and Joseph Smith, who held Trichinopoly, where the French prisoners exceeded his small garrison of invalids by five to one. Mahomed Yusuf, of Nellore, also did good service in partisan warfare against the French.

Lawrence's garrison comprised 1,600 Europeans (including officers), 64 Topasses, 89 Coffrees (natives of Madagascar and the East Coast of Africa), and 2,220 Sepoys. Nine hundred of the European infantry belonged to

Colonel Draper's regiment, the 79th, that had just arrived from England. There were also about 140 men of the Royal Artillery. The occupation of the town by Lally was the signal for the French troops to disperse themselves in search of plunder and drink. Their disorder and drunkenness being known in the fort, a sortie was determined on. Six hundred men with two field pieces were placed under Colonel Draper for the purpose. Draper entered the town, before he was discovered by the French, and put to flight those opposed to him. French reinforcements then came up, and a scene of much confusion followed. The English troops got separated, and Draper, with four men only, was in brief possession of a battery of French guns. Saubinet, one of Lally's best officers, was killed, and d'Estaing was taken prisoner; but the English were obliged to regain the fort in face of the additional reinforcements brought up by Lally, after suffering a loss of fifty killed, as many wounded, and 103 taken prisoners, besides six officers killed and three wounded. The French acknowledged a loss of 200 killed and wounded, besides four officers killed and twelve wounded. The loss of Saubinet and the capture of Count d'Estaing* were seriously felt by Lally at the opening of the siege.

On the 2nd January, the French batteries opened, and the siege was closely pressed. Sallies were made from time to time with more or less success. In one of them, Major Brereton, of the 79th, captured two guns, and brought them into the fort. A welcome supply of powder was brought in in a singular way. The French had dispatched three native boats laden with fifty barrels of powder, from Sadras, with a French soldier in each boat. The boatmen seized and disarmed the Frenchmen, and brought the powder into the fort, for which they were paid the full value.

On the 30th January, *The Shaftesbury*, East Indiaman, managed to run the gauntlet of the French blockading ships, and landed a much needed supply of treasure and warlike stores. Meanwhile, Caillaud, Preston and Mahomed Yusuf had carried on a daring and harassing warfare against the French communications. By great exertions, Caillaud had succeeded in

* After the siege, d'Estaing was released on parole. He broke his engagement, and assisted in destroying the Company's factory at Gombroon a few months later, much to the indignation of the Directors. He was again taken prisoner at sea, and brought to England.

raising a force of about 4,700 natives, with which he advanced and fought an indecisive action at S. Thomé on the 9th February. All this time the siege had been pressed by regular approaches, and the crisis was imminent; when, on the 16th February, Pocock's fleet sailed into the roadstead, a few hours before Lally's intended assault.

The condition of the garrison was so much better than that of the besiegers that it is doubtful if an assault would have been successful. Anyhow, Lally determined not to hazard it. He broke up his camp at once, and, the next morning, the retreating French columns were visible from the walls of the fort. Thus came to an end the most notable siege that had yet occurred in India, and the last serious bid for an Eastern Empire by the French. Fifty-two French guns and a quantity of stores were found in the trenches. The English loss amounted to 33 officers, 559 Europeans, and 346 Sepoys killed, wounded, and prisoners. The fort was so well supplied that it was calculated there were enough stores to stand another siege. All the operations of the defence had been managed by Lawrence. Mr. Pigot had had the good sense to abstain from interference, while he had been of much use in directing the distribution of supplies.

The reinforcements from England brought up the strength of European troops in Madras to over 1,700. The Council thought they ought to do something. Against Lawrence's advice, they sent him towards Conjeveram, which was occupied by Lally. But Lawrence's army was badly off for transport, and the Council found they had not money to maintain the troops in the field. They were now as anxious to bring back their troops to Madras, as they had been to send them out. Lawrence pointed out the evil of retreating in face of the enemy, though he had looked on the move towards Conjeveram as a mistake. To strengthen the Council's infirmity of purpose, he left the army and came to Madras. His health had completely broken down, and he made known his intention of returning to England. A few days later, in April, 1759, he sailed, with the intention of never returning to India. On his arrival in England, the Directors granted him an annuity of £500 a year. In September, 1760, the Directors voted statues to Lawrence, Clive, and Pocock "that their eminent and signal services to this Company may be ever had in remembrance."

On the 3rd October, 1761, Lawrence again took his seat in the Madras Council, having returned to India in the *Fox*, packet; yielding, apparently to the solicitation of the Directors. By this time, he had so thoroughly won their confidence that his position was greatly improved. He was again made Commander-in-Chief of all the Company's forces in India, and, to ensure that he should not be superseded in the field by any colonel of King's troops, he received the commission of Major-General in the East Indies, from the King. He was given a seat in Council at Madras, next to the Governor, with power to vote like any other member, instead of being restricted, as heretofore, to military subjects only. His salary was fixed at £1,500 a year, and it was ordered that, in the event of his visiting Bengal, or any other place where there was a Council, he was to be granted a seat on the Council Board; it being particularly mentioned that he was to take precedence of Colonel Coote.* Hitherto,

* In March, 1759, the Directors sent orders uniting the command of the King's and Company's troops in Bengal under Coote. At the same time, it was provided that, in the event of Coote's death, the nomination of his provisional successor was to be made by Lawrence, and was "on no pretence whatever" to be set aside by the civil authorities.

no personal staff had been granted to the senior military officer, except in the field. Lawrence was now granted an aide-de-camp and a brigade major. From this time his work was wholly administrative. The power of the French in India had been broken: Caillaud, Carnac, Coote and Adams were dealing effectively with the situation in Bengal.

One of the most serious things Lawrence had to deal with arose from the treachery of his old Brahmin interpreter. Since 1756 Mahomed Yusuf's loyalty had fallen under suspicion. In 1761, at the instance of the Council, the Nawab was induced to appoint him as Governor of Madura and Tinnevelly. Before long he began to give trouble, and it became evident that he aimed at independence. He collected arms and men, strengthened the fortifications of Madura, and, at the end of 1762, invaded Travancore territory without authority. Two months later he openly hoisted French colours, and was found to have over 25,000 men in his pay, among them being a corps of 200 Europeans under a French officer named Flamicourt. At the same time a certain M. Mandave, living at the Danish settlement of Tranquebar, announced himself as the representative of the French Government, and called on the Madras Council to desist from coercing Mahomed Yusuf. He asserted that Madura had been ceded to the French by Mahomed Yusuf, and that the cession must be recognised under the suspension of arms just concluded between the two nations; also, that Flamicourt was acting under his orders. The Madras Government was greatly embarrassed by these claims, but, on the Danish authorities being addressed, M. Mandave disavowed his connection with the French in Madura, and left India.

Lawrence advised immediate action, and a force of 9,900 men was assembled at Trichinopoly, under Colonel Monson, to march on Madura. Mahomed Yusuf's enterprising character quickly showed itself. On the 11th August he attacked a reconnoitring party of Sepoys, and drove it back with a loss of 150 men killed and wounded. On the 3rd September another reconnoitring party was driven back, with the loss of one European officer killed and sixteen or seventeen Europeans killed and wounded. Monson's artillery was so inferior that he was forced to raise the siege, in November, and take post six miles from

Madura. Mahomed Yusuf took advantage of the respite to open communication with the Governor and Lawrence, and liberal terms of amnesty were offered him; but he failed to take advantage of them. In April, 1764, the siege was renewed under Major Charles Campbell. On the 29th April, five redoubts were taken by storm. Batteries were opened, and, on 26th June, an assault was delivered and repulsed, with the loss of two officers killed and eight wounded; about 150 Europeans and fifty natives killed and wounded. Major Preston died of his wounds.

Campbell turned the siege into a blockade, which was strictly maintained, till scarcity and discontent forced the garrison to consider their own safety. Mahomed Yusuf was seized and confined by M. Marchand, the French commandant, who surrendered the place next day. On 15th October, Mahomed Yusuf was hanged as a rebel against the Nawab.

Lawrence's last years in India were probably the pleasantest of his life. He possessed the full confidence of the Directors in London and of his colleagues in Madras, and was united in bonds of the closest friendship with the Governor, Sir Robert Palk, to whom he stood second in the Council. In April, 1766, he bade a final farewell to India. He was succeeded, as Commander-in-Chief, by Caillaud; who, in turn, was succeeded by Joseph Smith. Mahomed Ali Khan, whose rule over the Carnatic had been secured by Lawrence's abilities, showed his gratitude by obtaining permission from the Company to grant Lawrence an annuity of 3,750 pagodas a year: about £1,500 in English money. The money was paid, through the Directors, till Lawrence's death, which took place in London on 10th January, 1775. His remains were conveyed to Dunchideock, near Exeter, where a monument was erected to him by Sir Robert Palk.

If the best General is the one who makes the fewest mistakes, Lawrence's name should occupy a high position on the list of commanders. To speak of him as a master of strategy would be out of place. There was little place for strategical developments in the warfare he was engaged in. His work was purely tactical. The Council kept all questions of strategy jealously in their own hands. But against Law and de Kerjean in 1752, and by his transfer of operations from Trivadi to

Trichinopoly in 1753, he showed a grasp of strategical principles that would have won success on a larger field. The armies he led were out of all proportion to the issues they decided. They were always of inferior quality. How bad they could be, at times, was shown at Volcondah, in April, 1751, during Lawrence's absence from India, when, with such officers as Clive, Dalton, and Kilpatrick, the European companies behaved in such a cowardly way that they had to be marched away from the field of operations. But Lawrence had that supreme gift of a great commander in being able to obtain great efforts from his men at critical moments, while he commanded their entire confidence at all times.

In the field, Lawrence exhibited all the qualities of a great commander, though opportunity to exercise them on a large scale was denied him. In front of the enemy, his self-possession never deserted him at the most trying moments. On no occasion did he ever hesitate or convene a council of war, as Clive did before Plassey. Never forcing a battle without necessity, he struck, with all his force and with the greatest daring, when the opportunity occurred. His decision once taken was carried out without faltering, and always with the best results. Especially had he the gift of misleading and confusing his enemy as to his intentions. In council, his judgment was as sound as it was in the field. Again and again the civil government had to repent that they had followed their own devices, and neglected Lawrence's advice. Yet with all this he seems never to have made a personal enemy. Among the prominent men of that time he stands alone in having left no trace of personal ill-feeling attached to his name.

Lawrence appears to have possessed one of those minds that, working in ordinary grooves, comes to the right conclusion under all circumstances, so easily and unerringly, that the world gives the name of Common Sense to what in a more showy personality it would have styled Genius. d'Auteuil, Law, de Kerjean, Astruc, Brenier, Astruc again, Maissin, Lally, every French leader who crossed swords with him, retired defeated from the combat, or had to yield himself a prisoner. Macaulay writes of Lawrence as being "gifted with no intellectual faculty higher than plain good sense," and leaves it to be inferred that Lawrence's triumph over Law was as much due to Clive as to his own efforts. In this he was no doubt misled by Clive's biographer, who writes of Clive "placing himself" under Lawrence when Lawrence returned to India in March, 1752. Clive had, at that time, only just sprung into notice by his feats at Arcot and Covripauk. His merits were challenged, and his successes were put down to luck. There was a strong feeling, in the army, of personal dislike to him, which found expression in an address to Lawrence. Had Clive refused to serve under Lawrence, he would have had no alternative but to abandon the military profession and return to his writership. Instead of Lawrence being indebted to Clive, it was Clive who, at that time, owed his advancement to Lawrence.

In the operations that crushed Law and d'Auteuil, Lawrence took Clive into his confidence and listened to his advice. That he should have done so, considering their difference of age and rank at the time, is a proof of the penetration of Lawrence's character. He certainly would have hesitated to divide his forces as he did, had he not gauged Law's over-caution and lack of enterprise, and had he not recognised Clive's capacity to carry out his views. But Clive made no move except under Lawrence's orders, though the fact that most of the fighting was done by him, causes his name to stand out more prominently than Lawrence's during the two months' campaign. After events showed that Lawrence was well able to act by himself. Clive was not at Bahoor, nor was he in India, when Lawrence fought Astruc and Brenier, Morari Rao and Hyder Ali, on the battlefields of Trichinopoly in 1753. The operations of that year alone are sufficient to establish Lawrence's reputation. Yet, for some reason not easily explained, Lawrence's military triumphs have been overshadowed by Clive's, though Clive was never matched against a French commander of any capacity. But the whole nature of the man was so quiet and unassuming, that his genuine merit might easily pass unobserved. Few things are more characteristic of Lawrence than his relations with Clive. When he arrived in India, totally ignorant of the country, at an age when most men adapt themselves with difficulty to novel circumstances, it would not have been surprising if he had regarded with some mistrust a masterful, headstrong, young man of twenty-two, who had only established at that time a reputation for love of fighting. But Lawrence quickly recognised Clive's genius, and reported to his superiors that Clive's successes were not due to good luck, as many imagined, but to real merit. When the expedition was prepared to avenge the horrors of the Black Hole of Calcutta, ill-health alone prevented Lawrence from taking the command. Lawrence, and not Clive, would have triumphed at Plassey, had Lawrence's health permitted him to assume the command.

Throughout his career in India, the relations of Lawrence with Clive, who quarrelled with almost everybody else, were of the most cordial description. When the East India Company voted a sword set with diamonds to Clive, he refused to receive it unless a similar honour was paid to Lawrence;* and, when Lawrence retired to England, Clive, who had become rich and powerful, bestowed on him an annuity

* The story of Clive refusing to receive the sword voted to him by the East India Company, unless one was also given to Lawrence, rests on the authority of Clive's biographer. It is indirectly supported by the imperfect records now in existence. Lawrence's sword was not voted to him till three months after a testimonial to Clive had been determined on, and then in such a manner as to show that it was an afterthought. It is remarkable also that, in repairing the oversight, the Directors voted a sword worth £750 to Lawrence, after granting one worth £500 to Clive, as if they had all at once become aware of Lawrence's superior claims. Clive was in London at the time, Lawrence being still in India.

LAWRENCE'S MONUMENT IN WESTMINSTER ABBEY.

[To face p. 119.

of £500 from his private purse. Nothing is more honourable to Clive than the deference and consideration with which he treated Lawrence at all times, and nothing testifies better to Lawrence's character than the ungrudging regard paid him by Clive.

Since Lawrence's day many illustrious names have been added to the roll of our Indian officers. None among them has a better claim to be remembered than Stringer Lawrence, the Father of the Indian Army.

On his death, the Directors of the East India Company voted a sum of £700 for the erection of a monument to his memory, in Westminster Abbey, in testimony of their gratitude for his eminent services. It bears the following legend :—

DISCIPLINE ESTABLISHED.
FORTRESSES PROTECTED.
SETTLEMENTS EXTENDED.
FRENCH
AND INDIAN ARMIES
DEFEATED
AND
PEACE CONCLUDED
IN THE CARNATIC.

With a carved representation of the fortified rock of Trichinopoly.

APPENDIX A

THE PARENTAGE OF STRINGER LAWRENCE.

THE only positive knowledge we have of Stringer Lawrence's parentage is from the baptismal register in the Church of All Saints at Hereford, which shows that on 27th February, 1697–98, was baptised Stringer, the son of Mr. John Lawrence and Mary, his wife. In the All Saints' burial register is recorded the burial of Michael Stringer on 13th November, 1698. It is reasonable to presume that Stringer was the maiden name of Lawrence's mother.

The coat of arms on Stringer Lawrence's monument in Westminster Abbey (ermine, a cross ragulé gules) is almost identical with the coat of arms granted to Sir John Lawrence, Alderman of London, and Lord Mayor in 1664, in which year the grant of arms was made (ermine, a cross ragulé gules, a canton ermines).

The archives of the City of Hereford, which were partly destroyed in the Civil War, show that there was one or more families of the name of Lawrence living in Hereford in the seventeenth and eighteenth centuries.

In 1625 James Lawrence was Mayor of Hereford.

A memorandum signed by the Parliamentary officer, Colonel John Birch, shows that "Mr. Lawrence" was fined six pounds for being disaffected to Parliament.

In 1660 James Lawrence, junior, gentleman, was admitted to the freedom of the city, and became Mayor in the following year.

In 1682 John Lawrence, apothecary, and in 1702 John Lawrence, brewer, were admitted to the freedom of the city. One of these must, almost certainly, have been the father of Stringer Lawrence.

In 1707 William Lawrence, brewer; in 1714 Humphries Lawrence, gentleman, of Leominster; in 1761 Samuel Lawrence, brewer, were admitted to the freedom of the city.

APPENDIX B

SOOBADARS OF THE DECCAN, AND NAWABS OF THE CARNATIC IN THE EIGHTEENTH CENTURY.

SOOBADARS OF THE DECCAN.

A.D.

1691—Zulfikar Khan. Nusrut Jung.

Aurungzib's General: son of Assad Khan (Meer Jumla): recalled 1702.

1702—Daood Khan, Punnee.

Zulfikar Khan's deputy and successor: recalled 1713.

1713—Chin Killij Khan, Asaf Jah, Nizam-ool-Moolk.

Son of Ghazi-oo-deen Khan, Moghul noble. On his appointment, Arcot made into a separate Nawabship. Makes himself independent 1720: reconciled to the Emperor 1722: goes finally to the Deccan 1741: dies 1748.

1748—Nazir Jung.

Son of Nizam-ool-Moolk: seizes the throne: imprisons Mozuffer Jung: assassinated on the field of battle against the French, 16th December, 1750.

1750—Mozuffer Jung.

Son of Nizam-ool-Moolk's daughter, and designed by him as his successor. Appointed by firman from the Emperor, and supported by the French, who proclaim him Soobadar of the Deccan after Nazir Jung's death: killed by the Nawab of Kurnool, February, 1751.

1751—SALABUT JUNG.

Son of Nizam-ool-Moolk: proclaimed Nizam by the French: imprisoned by Nizam Ali 1761: murdered 1763.

1761—NIZAM ALI.

Son of Nizam-ool-Moolk: rebels against Salabut Jung: is reconciled: rebels again, and seizes the throne 1761: dies August, 1803.

NAWABS OF THE CARNATIC.

A.D.

Arcot made into a separate Nawabship 1713. (See Soobadars of the Deccan.)

1713—SAADUT-OOLLAH KHAN.

Daood Khan's Foujdar and Dewan: dies 1732.

1732—DOST ALI KHAN.

Nephew and adopted son of Saadut-oollah Khan: slain in battle with the Mahrattas.

1742—SUFDER ALI KHAN.

Son of Dost Ali Khan: assassinated, 1742, by Moortis Ali Khan, his cousin and brother-in-law.

Nawabship claimed by Moortis Ali Khan, supported by the French: allegiance refused by subordinate Chiefs, who set up Mahomed Said Khan, son of Sufder Ali Khan. Mahomed Said Khan set aside by the Nizam: assassinated by Pathans 1744.

1743—KHOJAH ABDULLAH.

Nizam's General appointed: poisoned by Anwaroodeen.

1744—ANWAROODEEN.

Nizam's Governor of Ellore appointed: slain in battle at Amboor, 1749, against Mozuffer Jung and Chunda Sahib, supported by the French.

1749—MAHOMED ALI KHAN. WALLAH JAH.

Son of Anwaroodeen, appointed by the Nizam, and supported by the English: holds the Nawabship till his death. A firman of the Emperor acknowledges the independence of the Carnatic 1765: dies 1795.

CHUNDA SAHIB.

Dost Ali Khan's Dewan, claims Nawabship on Anwaroodeen's death: supported by Nizam's brother, Mozuffer Jung, and by the French: assassinated by Tanjore General 1752. On his death, Dupleix claims the Nawabship for himself, in virtue of a sunnud obtained from the Nizam Salabut Jung during Chunda Sahib's lifetime. On the strength of this, Dupleix proclaims Reza (Rajah) Sahib, son of Chunda Sahib, 1752, but a few months later sets him aside, and proclaims Moortis Ali Khan. Moortis Ali Khan makes submission to Mahomed Ali Khan, 1754. Lally again appoints Reza Sahib 1759.

1795—UMDAT-OOL-OOMRA.

Son of Mahomed Ali Khan: dies July, 1801.

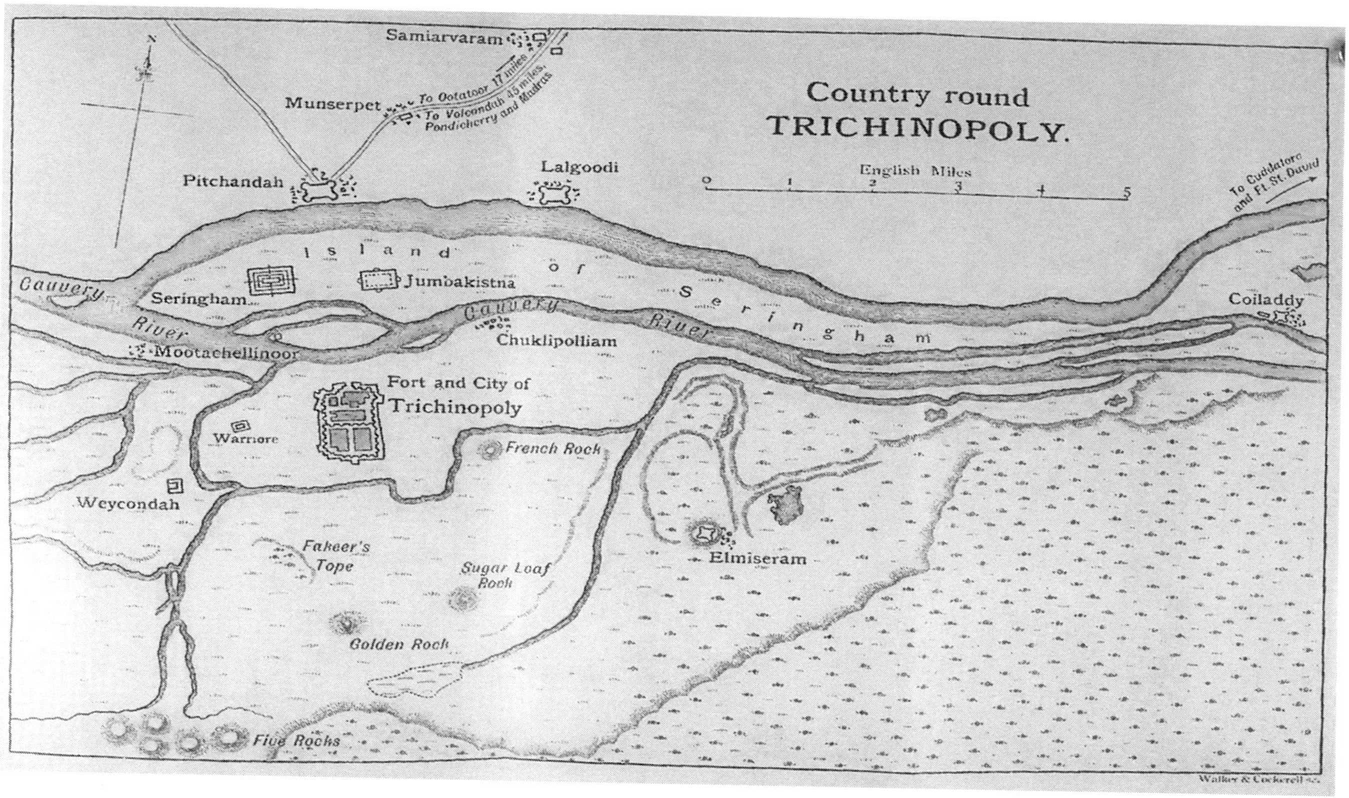
Country round
TRICHINOPOLY.
English Miles
0 1 2 3 4 5
N
Samiarvaram
Munserpet
To Ootatoor 17 miles
To Volcondah 45 miles, Pondicherry and Madras
Pitchandah
Lalgoodi
To Cuddalore and Ft. St. David
Island of Seringham
Seringham
Jumbakistna
Cauvery
River
Cauvery River
Coiladdy
Chuklipolliam
Mootachellinoor
Fort and City of
Trichinopoly
Warriore
Weycondah
French Rock
Fakeer's Tope
Sugar Loaf Rock
Golden Rock
Elmiseram
Five Rocks
Walker & Cockerell sc.

INDEX